Contents

List of resources 3
Introduction 4
How to use the CD-ROM 5

D0452385

dup

Places of worship PAGE 7
Notes on the CD-ROM resources 8
Notes on the photocopiable pages 17
Photocopiable pages 18

Christianity PAGE 21
Notes on the CD-ROM resources 21
Notes on the photocopiable pages 26
Photocopiable pages 27

Judaism PAGE 32
Notes on the CD-ROM resources 32
Notes on the photocopiable pages 36
Photocopiable pages 37

Islam PAGE 42
Notes on the CD-ROM resources 42
Notes on the photocopiable pages 46
Photocopiable pages 47

Hinduism PAGE 52
Notes on the CD-ROM resources 52
Notes on the photocopiable pages 55
Photocopiable pages 56

Sikhism PAGE 61
Notes on the CD-ROM resources 61
Notes on the photocopiable pages 65
Photocopiable pages 66

Buddhism PAGE 69
Notes on the CD-ROM resources 69
Notes on the photocopiable pages 72
Photocopiable pages 74

Licence

IMPORTANT – PERMITTED USE AND WARNINGS – READ CAREFULLY BEFORE USING

Text © 2006 Lynne Broadbent
© 2006 Scholastic Ltd

Published by Scholastic Ltd, Villiers House,
Clarendon Avenue, Leamington Spa,
Warwickshire CV32 5PR

Printed by Bell & Bain Ltd, Glasgow

3 4 5 6 7 8 9 0   7 8 9 0 1 2 3 4 5

British Library Cataloguing-in-Publication Data
A catalogue record for this book is available from
the British Library.

ISBN 0-439-96538-1
978-0439-96538-5

Visit our website at
www.scholastic.co.uk

CD developed in association with
Footmark Media Ltd

Author
Lynne Broadbent

Project Editor
Wendy Tse

Editor
Sally Gray

Assistant Editors
Victoria Lee and Niamh O'Carroll

Series Designer
Joy Monkhouse

Designer
Erik Ivens

Cover photographs
© Photodisc
© Articles of Faith
© Ingram
© Comstock

Acknowledgements

With thanks to: All Saints Parish Church, Leamington Spa; Articles of Faith; BFSS National RE Centre; Birmingham Progressive Synagogue; Clear Vision Trust, Manchester; Delhi Musical Stores; Federation Kosher; Guru Amardas Gurdwara, Leicester; Harrow Central Mosque; Holy Trinity Church, Leamington Spa; Masjid Tabuk & Evington Muslim Centre, Leicester; The Movement for Reform Judaism; Leicester Orthodox Synagogue; Shree Krishna Temple, Leamington Spa; Shree Sanatan Mandir, Leicester; St Andrew's Church, Aylestone.

Extracts from In the Prophet's Garden: A Selection of ahadith for the young compiled by Fatima M D'Oyen and Abdelkader Chachi © 2002, Islamic Foundation. Extracts from the National Curriculum for England © Crown copyright material is reproduced with the permission of the Controller of HMSO and the Queen's Printer for Scotland. Extracts from Religious Education: The non-statutory national framework © 2004, Qualification and Curriculum Authority (2004, QCA and DfES).

Every effort has been made to trace copyright holders and the publishers apologise for any omissions.

Made with Macromedia is a trademark of
Macromedia, Inc. Director ®
Copyright © 1984–2000 Macromedia, Inc.

Minimum Specifications:
PC: Windows 98 SE or higher
Processor: Pentium 2 (or equivalent) 400 MHz
RAM: 128 Mb
CD-ROM drive: 48x (52x preferred)

MAC: OS 9.2 (OSX preferred)
Processor: G3 400 MHz
RAM: 128 Mb

List of resources on the CD-ROM

The page numbers refer to the teacher's notes provided in this book.

Places of worship

A world map	8
Map of Israel/Palestine	8
Map of India	8
Video: What a church is like	8
A traditional church	8
Worship in a church	8
Coventry Cathedral	8
Inside Coventry Cathedral	8
Church of the Nativity in Bethelem	9
Basilica of the Annunciation in Nazareth	9
Tomb at the Garden of Gethsemane in Jerusalem	9
Shabbat in the family home	10
Video: What a synagogue is like	11
A synagogue	11
Torah Scrolls in the Ark	11
The Western Wall at Jersualem	11
Worshipping at the Western Wall	11
Muslims praying at home	12
Video: What a mosque is like	12
A mosque	12
Praying in a mosque	12
Ladies' prayer room	12
The Ka'bah at Makkah	13
Hindu shrine in the home	13
Video: What a mandir is like	14
A mandir	14
Inside a mandir	14
Hindus worshipping at the River Ganges	14
Video: What a gurdwara is like	14
A gurdwara	14
Worship in the gurdwara	14
The Golden Temple at Amritsar	15
Buddhist shrine in the home	16
Video: Inside a Buddhist centre	16
Giant Buddha statue	16

Christianity

A picture of Jesus	21
A mosaic of Christ Pantocrator	21
Jesus' baptism	22
Jesus in the temple at 12 years old	22
Temptations of Christ	23
Jesus overturns the moneychangers' tables	23
Last Supper	24
Crucifixion	24
Video: The Eucharist	25
Empty cross	25
Easter garden	25
Video: Why Christmas is special	25
Video: Why Easter is special	25

Judaism

Video: Using the Torah in the synagogue	32
Mezuzah cases and mezuzah scroll	33
Audio: The Shema	33
Kosher foods	34
Bar Mitzvah	34
Bat Mitzvah	34
Simchat Torah	35
Celebrating Simchat Torah	35
Celebrating Shavuot	35

Islam

99 names of Allah	42
The Qur'an	43
Audio: The Shahadah	43
Picture of the Shahadah	43
Video: Salah – prayer in Islam	44
Video: What is Zakat?	44
Ramadan	45
Map of Hajj	45

Hinduism

Video: Worship in the mandir	52
Ganesh	53
Krishna as a baby	53
Lord Krishna & Radha	54
Video: Worshipping Lord Krishna	54
Shiva	54

Sikhism

Guru Nanak	61
Guru Gobind Singh	61
Video: The five Ks	64
Photograph of the five Ks	64
Video: Turban tying	62
Amrit	62
The Nishan Sahib	63
The Nishan Sahib and Baisakhi	63
Guru Granth Sahib, the holy book	63
Guru Granth Sahib being put to bed	63
Audio: A kirtan	64
Harmonium and tablas	64
Video: Harmonium being played	64
Video: Tablas being played	64
Langar	64

Buddhism

A small Buddha statue	69
Video: What do Buddhists promise?	70
Wesak – a Buddhist festival	70
Prayer flags in the mountains	71
A prayer flag	71

INTRODUCTION

This book and CD-ROM support teaching and learning in religious education for Key Stage 2 children. The legal requirement for teaching religious education in county schools is the LEA-Agreed Syllabus, with Diocesan Syllabuses supporting teaching and learning in Church schools. These syllabuses have common features, such as teaching about homes and families, celebrations, special places of worship and special books and stories. The non-statutory framework for religious education echoes these features in its themes of 'religion', 'family and community', 'worship' and 'authority'.

The CD-ROM provides a large bank of visual and aural resources around these themes. The book provides background information, ideas for discussion and activities to accompany the CD resources. All have been specifically chosen to meet the requirements for resources identified in Agreed Syllabuses for Years 3 to 6. Also included are photocopiable resources that enable teachers to develop and broaden these areas of study if they wish. For example, activity sheets help children to clarify their thinking or to record what they find out.

The resources and their accompanying activities address the two distinct attainment targets of the non-statutory framework for religious education: Learning about religion and Learning from religion.

'Learning about religion' engages children in enquiry into, and investigation of, religion through the reading of religious stories, through meeting people from different faith communities, through visiting places of worship and through learning about festivals and celebrations.

'Learning from religion' is concerned with developing the children's capacity to reflect on their own experiences and to respond to what they have learned. For example, reflecting on the celebrations which take place in their own homes or on their personal sense of belonging to a community, whether religious or secular.

Both 'Learning about religion' and 'Learning from religion' involve the development of investigation skills, as well as requiring the children to develop the capacity to reflect. The children will also develop skills in using the correct religious words and will be encouraged to recognise the similarities and differences in beliefs and practice.

Links with other subjects

English
There are many opportunities to read or tell stories about key figures from the different faiths covered in this book. The children can role-play and 'hot seat' story characters, as well as question members of faith communities. Religious education makes a significant contribution to the development of children's literacy and speaking and listening skills.

PSHE and citizenship
In religious education, children will develop their skills of communication, namely listening to others and sharing their own views and opinions. They will learn about the diverse communities within their local and international community, and about the similarities and differences in practices of worship.

Art and design
Religion makes a rich contribution to the arts through painting, stained glass windows, complex Islamic patterns and the symbolic design of its places of worship. Children will have opportunities to learn from encounters with the visual arts and from engaging with creative activities, such as the design of pictures and collages.

Music
Religions draw on a wide range of music and song in celebration and worship. The audio resources provide, for example, the opportunity to listen to the sounds of traditional Sikh music and to recognise the instruments used.

Geography
Children will learn about key religious sites and places of pilgrimage in different parts of the world, and will consult maps to identify their location.

HOW TO USE THE CD-ROM

Windows NT users

If you use Windows NT you may see the following error message: 'The procedure entry point Process32First could not be located in the dynamic link library KERNEL32.dll'. Click on **OK** and the CD will autorun with no further problems.

Setting up your computer for optimal use

On opening, the CD will alert you if changes are needed in order to operate the CD at its optimal use. There are three changes you may be advised to make:

Viewing resources at their maximum screen size

To see images at their maximum screen size, your screen display needs to be set to 800 x 600 pixels. In order to adjust your screen size you will need to **Quit** the program.

If using a PC, open the **Control Panel**. Select **Display** and then **Settings**. Adjust the **Desktop Area** to 800 x 600 pixels. Click on **OK** and then restart the program.

If using a Mac, from the **Apple** menu select **Control Panels** and then **Monitors** to adjust the screen size.

Adobe Acrobat Reader

To print high-quality versions of images and to view and print the photocopiable pages on the CD you need **Adobe Acrobat Reader** installed on your computer. If you do not have it installed already, a version is provided on the CD. To install this version **Quit** the 'Ready Resources' program.

If using a PC, right-click on the **Start** menu on your desktop and choose **Explore**. Click on the + sign to the left of the CD drive entitled 'Ready Resources' and open the folder called 'Acrobat Reader Installer'. Run the program in this folder to install **Adobe Acrobat Reader**.

If using a Mac, double-click on the 'Ready Resources' icon on the desktop and on the 'Acrobat Reader Installer' folder. Run the program contained in this folder to install **Adobe Acrobat Reader**.

PLEASE NOTE: If you do not have **Adobe Acrobat Reader** installed, you will not be able to print high-quality versions of images, or to view or print photocopiable pages (although these are provided in this book and can be photocopied).

It is recommended you use **Adobe Acrobat Reader** to zoom in to focus on specific areas.

QuickTime

In order to view the videos and listen to the audio on this CD you will need to have **QuickTime version 5** or later installed on your computer. If you do not have it installed already, or have an older version of **QuickTime**, the latest version can be downloaded at http://www.apple.com/quicktime/download/win.html. If you choose to install this version, **Quit** the 'Ready Resources' program.

PLEASE NOTE: If you do not have **QuickTime** installed you will be unable to view the films.

Menu screen

▶ Click on the **Resource Gallery** of your choice to view the resources available under that topic.

▶ Click on **Complete Resource Gallery** to view all the resources available on the CD.

▶ Click on **Photocopiable Resources (PDF format)** to view a list of the photocopiables provided in this book.

▶ **Back**: click to return to the **opening screen**. Click **Continue** to move to the **Menu screen**.

▶ **Quit**: click to close the menu program and progress to the **Quit screen**. If you quit from the **Quit screen** you will exit the CD. If you do not quit you will return to the **Menu screen**.

Resource Galleries

▶ **Help**: click **Help** to find support on accessing and using images.

▶ **Back to menu**: click here to return to the **Menu screen**.

▶ **Quit**: click here to move to the **Quit screen** – see **Quit** above.

Viewing images

Small versions of each image are shown in the Resource Gallery. Click and drag the slider on the slide bar to scroll through the images in the Resource Gallery, or click on the arrows to move the images frame by frame. Roll the pointer over an image to see the caption.

▶ Click on an image to view the screen-sized version of it.

▶ To return to the Resource Gallery click on **Back to Resource Gallery**.

Viewing videos

Click on the video icon of your choice in the Resource Gallery. In order to view the videos on this CD, you will need to have **QuickTime** installed on your computer (see 'Setting up your computer for optimal use' above).

Once at the video screen, use the buttons on the bottom of the video screen to operate the video. The slide bar can be used for a fast forward and rewind. To return to the Resource Gallery click on **Back to Resource Gallery**.

Listening to sound recordings

Click on the required sound icon. Use the buttons or the slide bar to hear the sound. A transcript will be displayed on the viewing screen where appropriate. To return to the Resource Gallery, click on **Back to Resource Gallery**.

Printing

Click on the image to view it (see 'Viewing images' above). There are two print options:

1. **Print using Acrobat** enables you to print a high-quality version of an image. Choosing this option means that the image will open as a read-only page in **Adobe Acrobat** and in order to access these files you will need to have already installed **Adobe Acrobat Reader** on your computer (see 'Setting up your computer for optimal use' above). To print the selected resource, select **File** and then **Print**. Once you have printed the resource **minimise** or **close** the Adobe screen using – or **X** in the top right-hand corner of the screen. Return to the Resource Gallery by clicking on **Back to Resource Gallery**.

2. **Simple print** enables you to print a lower-quality version of the image without the need to use **Adobe Acrobat Reader**. Select the image and click on the **Simple print** option. After printing, click on **Back to Resource Gallery**.

Slideshow presentation

If you would like to present a number of resources without having to return to the Resource Gallery and select a new image each time, you can compile a slideshow. Click on the + tabs at the top of each image in the Resource Gallery you would like to include in your presentation (pictures, sound and video can be included). It is important that you click on the images in the order in which you would like to view them (a number will appear on each tab to confirm the order). If you would like to change the order, click on **Clear slideshow** and begin again. Once you have selected your images (up to a maximum of 20), click on **Play slideshow** and you will be presented with the first of your selected resources. To move to the next selection in your slideshow click on **Next slide**, to see a previous resource click on **Previous slide**. You can end your slideshow presentation at any time by clicking on **Resource Gallery**. Your slideshow selection will remain selected until you **Clear slideshow** or return to the **Menu screen**.

Viewing on an interactive whiteboard or data projector

Resources can be viewed directly from the CD. To make viewing easier for a whole class, use a large monitor, data projector or interactive whiteboard. For group, paired or individual work, the resources can be viewed from the computer screen.

Photocopiable resources (PDF format)

To view or print a photocopiable resource page, click on the required title in the list and the page will open as a read-only page in **Adobe Acrobat**. In order to access these files you will need to have already installed **Adobe Acrobat Reader** on your computer (see 'Setting up your computer for optimal use' above). To print the selected resource select **File** and then **Print**. Once you have printed the resource **minimise** or **close** the Adobe screen using – or **X** in the top right-hand corner of the screen. This will take you back to the list of PDF files. To return to the **Menu screen**, click on **Back**.

PLACES OF WORSHIP

Content and skills

This chapter addresses the theme of worship in the home and neighbourhood as well as worship through pilgrimage to places of special significance throughout the world. Pilgrimage is not viewed in the same way by all faith traditions and it is only in Islam that pilgrimage is one of five requirements for believers. However, people of all religious traditions will have a spiritual bond with places where key figures lived and died, or where buildings of historical importance are located, and a visit to these places will be part of their own personal pilgrimage or spiritual quest.

The theme of worship encourages exploration of how beliefs are expressed through ritual, by the individual believer, and by the local and global communities. The theme lies at the heart of religious practice and will be found in all locally agreed syllabuses for Religious Education and is identified in the non-statutory framework for Religious Education as a theme to be addressed with Key Stage 2 pupils.

In this chapter the children will be investigating religion through the collection of evidence from a wide range of sources including maps, directories and interviews with members of faith communities; they will develop their ability to use words and phrases associated with worship and will be able to describe the impact of religion on people's lives.

The Resource Gallery for 'Places of worship' on the CD-ROM, together with the teachers' notes and photocopiable pages in this chapter, support teaching and learning about worship. The teachers' notes contain background information about the resources and include ways of using them as a whole class, for group work or by individual pupils. Some of the activities link with other areas of the curriculum, such as literacy and art and design. Wherever possible, the activities encourage the children to ask questions and develop an enquiring approach to their learning.

Resources on the CD-ROM

The resources include maps illustrating the places of origin of a range of faith traditions and video footage of places of worship within the United Kingdom. There are also photographs that show how people worship at home and within the place of worship, and photographs of sites of religious interest and pilgrimage around the world. These resources serve to develop the children's understanding of the concept of worship as well as placing each religion within a global context.

Photocopiable pages

The photocopiable pages in the book are also provided in PDF format on the CD-ROM and can be printed from there. They include:
▶ word cards containing essential vocabulary for the unit
▶ word cards that explore sacred places and their origins
▶ an activity sheet on places of worship.

NOTES ON THE CD-ROM RESOURCES

A world map, Map of Israel/Palestine, Map of India

This map shows the United Kingdom and the places in the world identified in this chapter as key sites for different faith communities. Israel, also known as the land of Palestine, a country of pilgrimage for Jews, Christians and Muslims can be seen on the edge of the Mediterranean Sea and on the boundary of Asia and Africa; Makkah in Saudi Arabia is a place of pilgrimage or hajj for Muslims; India is the 'birthplace' of Hinduism, Buddhism and Sikhism, while neighbouring countries such as China, Tibet and Thailand are countries of significant Buddhist expansion.

Israel, formerly part of Palestine, is a place of pilgrimage for Jews, Christians and Muslims. The Western Wall in Jerusalem, often referred to as the Wailing Wall is all that remains of the Temple that was used in biblical times, and is now regarded as a holy place for Jews. For Christians, Israel is a place of pilgrimage – Bethlehem being the birthplace of Jesus, Nazareth the place where he is believed to have grown up and Jerusalem the place of Jesus' crucifixion. For Muslims, Jerusalem marks the site of the Dome of the Rock, an early mosque built over a rock from which Muslims believe that Muhammad went up to heaven and returned with teaching about prayer.

Hinduism, one of the oldest religions, developed in India. The River Ganges, a sacred river for Hindus, flows down from the Himalayan mountains which are regarded as the 'home of the gods'.

Discussing the maps

▶ Talk to the children about places that are special to them, including different parts of the world with which they may have links (such as family living in different countries).
▶ Remind the children about key religious places such as Makkah and Bethlehem.
▶ Discuss how most religions have a special place in the world, which may be the birthplace of a key figure or the place where a key event happened.
▶ Identify the countries on the world map that have particular religious associations. Look at their differences in size and their locations in relation to the United Kingdom and to each other.
▶ Identify the key places for Jews, Christians and Muslims on the map of Israel/Palestine.

Activities

▶ Use the 'Sacred places word cards' (photocopiable page 19) to mark key places (and the events that took place in them) for Jews, Christians and Muslims.
▶ Invite a Jew, Christian, or Muslim who has visited a special place of worship outside the United Kingdom to speak to the children about their experiences.
▶ Collect travel brochures for Israel and India, and look at the types of holiday advertised.
▶ Make travel brochures for either Israel or India, focusing on the pilgrimage sites.
▶ Plan a journey or holiday to Israel based on what a person of each religion would find of interest.

CHRISTIANITY

Video: What a church is like, A traditional church, Worship in a church, Coventry Cathedral, Inside Coventry Cathedral

The video and photograph of a church show the exterior and interior of a church built in a traditional cruciform style. A church is built in the shape of a cross as a reminder of Jesus and his death on the cross. A cross can be seen on the roof of the church identifying it as a Christian place of worship. Inside, the altar, the most important part of the building, faces towards the east (towards the rising sun as a symbol of the resurrection). Other features visible are the choir, the lectern, on which the Bible rests, and the pews for the congregation. There is also a Mary and Child icon.

For Christians, 'the church' is not really the church building, but the people for it is they who live out the teaching of Jesus in the world. The photograph 'Worship in a church' shows people waiting to take Holy Communion (the bread and the wine) from the priest; others are singing a hymn from their hymn books. Praying, singing and listening to the reading of the Bible are all ways in which Christians worship God.

A cathedral is the main church in a diocese (an area under a bishop's care) and many cities have one. Some cathedrals are very big, such as St Paul's Cathedral in London, but others are quite small, such as the cathedrals in Birmingham and Manchester. Some cathedrals are famous for particular events. Canterbury Cathedral in Kent is the place where Thomas Becket, then Archbishop of Canterbury, was murdered. It has been a pilgrimage site for many centuries and is the subject of Chaucer's Canterbury Tales.

Coventry Cathedral was bombed during the Second World War and a new cathedral was built next to the old one, with an archway joining the old and new buildings, as shown in the photograph. The building is therefore a symbol of resurrection, with the old giving rise to the new. The photograph 'Inside Coventry Cathedral' shows people worshipping in a Pentecostal service.

Discussing the video and photographs
▶ Talk about the different types of church in which Christians worship.
▶ Ask the children about the churches they have seen or visited locally.
▶ Discuss with the children what they can see Christians doing as part of their worship.
▶ Discuss the belief that 'the church' is really the people and not the church building.

Activities
▶ Make a display of churches and cathedrals from around Britain. Look at the similarities and differences between the churches and cathedrals.
▶ Plot the position of churches and/or cathedrals close to the school on a local map. Make a guidebook about the local church or churches for other children who might make a visit.
▶ Visit one local church and compare it with those shown in the photograph. A Baptist or Methodist church might look very different.
▶ Look at some examples of hymns and prayers that might be sung or said during worship in a church. For example, the hymn 'O Jesus I have promised' is often sung as a commitment to Christian belief, while 'The Lord's Prayer' is usually said in services.
▶ Look at the church noticeboard for activities that a church might offer to the community, such as clubs for the aged or playgroups for young children. These form part of the Christian service to others in the local community.
▶ Invite a priest, minister or member of a local Christian community to speak to the children about their favourite hymns and prayers.

Church of the Nativity in Bethlehem, Basilica of the Annunciation in Nazareth, Tomb at the Garden of Gethsemane in Jerusalem

The Church of the Nativity in Bethlehem is recognisable from the Bell tower to the right of the picture. Although this is a large church, the entrance is very small – a group of people can be seen seated outside. The actual birthplace of Jesus is believed to be here and is marked by a star within the church crypt. Pilgrims come here and may say a prayer in this special place.

The 20th century basilica is found in Nazareth (the place where Jesus grew up). Above the door is an inscription in Latin, which means, 'The Word is made flesh and lives among us', referring to the Word of God, made flesh in the person of Jesus, who lives on among women and men. On either side of the window above the great door are carvings of the Gospel writers, Matthew, Mark, Luke and John. Inside the church, high on the walls, are mosaics from all over the world showing images of Mary and the child, Jesus.

This tomb is in the Garden of Gethsemane in Jerusalem. It is not the site of Jesus' burial but may be very like the tomb in which Jesus' body was placed after the crucifixion. The tomb is hewn out of the rock face and it is possible to walk inside the tomb into a small room with a ledge at one end on which the body was placed. Although there is now a door on the tomb, originally a large boulder would have been rolled in front of the entrance to seal the tomb. The small 'wall' which runs in front of the entrance would have provided a ridge to hold the boulder in place. On the modern door the words, 'He is not here he has been raised again...' are a reminder of the words in Matthew's Gospel (28:6). Many Christians hold services at this site as it helps them to think about what happened on the first Easter morning when Jesus' followers went to the tomb and found that his body had gone.

Discussing the photographs

▶ Discuss the things that can be seen in each picture which show that these sites are important to Christians.

▶ Talk about the times of the year that are important to the members of different religions. Discuss when pilgrims might try to visit each site, for example, Bethlehem at Christmas and the Garden Tomb at Easter.

▶ Discuss with the children the reasons why Christians might have wanted to build churches on these sites and why pilgrims want to visit them. How might pilgrims be changed by their visits?

Activities

▶ Use these photographs of the three important Christian sites in Israel with the map of Israel/Palestine (provided on the CD). Link them to the appropriate places on the map.

▶ Using a children's Bible, read the passages in Luke's Gospel that are linked to each site – 2:1-20 (birth of Jesus); 2:39-40 (Jesus, Mary and Joseph return to Nazareth); 23:55 (Jesus is laid in his tomb); 24 (Jesus is resurrected).

▶ Look at paintings of the Mother and Child and devise a Mother and Child image in mosaic like those in the church in Nazareth.

JUDAISM

Shabbat in the family home

The photograph shows worship in a family home. The table is set for the Friday Shabbat meal and the woman (possibly the mother), is welcoming Shabbat into the home. She does this just before sunset by lighting at least two candles – in this home, four candles have been lit. The mother will say the blessing for Shabbat to welcome it into the home: 'Blessed are You O Lord our God, King of the Universe, who commands us to light the Sabbath lights.' In a Jewish home, Shabbat is welcomed like a bride – hence a white tablecloth. On the table the wine for Kiddush can be seen. Everyone will have a cup of wine and the father will say Kiddush: 'Blessed are You O Lord our God, King of the Universe, Creator of the fruit of the vine.' Then everyone sips the sweet Sabbath wine, or red grape juice. The challah, two Sabbath loaves, will then be blessed with the words: 'Blessed are You O Lord our God, King of the Universe, who brings forth bread from the earth.' In this photograph, the challah are under the decorated white cover, to the right of the picture.

Discussing the photograph

▶ Discuss what can be seen that indicates that this is a special occasion.

▶ Discuss how having lit the candles, the woman will often 'draw' the light of the candles towards her.

▶ Talk together about the other items on the Shabbat table and why they are important in the celebration.

▶ Discuss the words of the blessings and how they convey a Jewish belief in God as a Creator.

Activities

▶ In the classroom, set a table ready for Shabbat. Choose children to act as the mother and father of the family. Ask them to describe the things that are said and done and the blessings that welcome Shabbat. While the children can say the blessings which would be said in a Jewish home and learn what the blessings mean, it is important that this is not seen as mimicking, or pretending to be Jewish.

▶ Ask the children to identify the things in their lives which they would count as 'blessings'. Make a visual display of these things.

▶ Discuss with the children how Jews keep Shabbat as a day of rest by not watching television, answering the telephone or going shopping. Discuss with the children the pros and cons of having a day of rest to spend with the family.

Video: What a synagogue is like, A synagogue, Torah scrolls in the Ark

The video shows the exterior and interior of an Orthodox synagogue. The interior view shows the Ark in which the Torah scrolls are kept. The photograph shows a modern building; it is recognisable as a synagogue from the outside by the menorah, a seven-branched candlestick, on the front wall.

In the photograph 'Torah scrolls in the Ark', the scrolls are dressed in blue velvet coverings, decorated with the Star of David, a menorah, and with symbols of the tablets of stone on which the Ten Commandments were written. Silver bells top the wooden rollers and, on two of the scrolls, a 'yad' can be seen. A 'yad', literally a 'hand', is a silver pointer used to point to the Hebrew words as the scroll is read (to avoid smudging the words which are handwritten in ink). The *ner tamid* lamp hangs in front of the Ark, and the light is a symbol of God's presence.

Discussing the video and photographs
▶ Ask the children to describe what they can see in the video and two photographs.
▶ Talk to the children about the 'clues' which would suggest that the building belongs to the Jewish faith.
▶ Discuss why the Torah scrolls might be so richly covered and decorated.

Activities
▶ Look on a map to identify the location of the nearest synagogue.
▶ Visit a local synagogue to look at the Torah scrolls.
▶ Read some of the stories found in the Torah, such as the story of Abraham and Isaac; Joseph and his brothers; or Moses leading the Hebrews out of slavery in Egypt (a story which is read in Jewish homes every year at Passover).
▶ Look at the Ten Commandments (see photocopiable page 40). Discuss the relevance of these commandments for people today.
▶ Talk to the children about different sources of guidance, and who or what guides them in the decisions they make. The word 'Torah' means 'teaching' – Jews believe that the scripture teaches how to worship God and how to treat others.

The Western Wall at Jerusalem, Worshipping at the Western Wall

The Western Wall at Jerusalem is the only remaining part of the Temple which was the holiest place for Jews. It is sometimes called the Wailing Wall as pilgrims often mourn the loss of their Temple. Many Jews come from all over the world to hold their Bar Mitzvahs at the Western Wall. Above the Wall can be seen the Dome of the Rock which is a holy place for Muslims and this shows the proximity of the two religious sites which in the past have led to conflict. The photograph 'Worshipping at the Western Wall' shows Jews praying at the Wall. All have their heads covered, many with their prayer shawls; some are reading from prayer books. Many Jews place written prayers in the cracks in the Wall.

Discussing the photographs
▶ Talk about the different things that make places special – for example, the birthplace of a key person or the site of a particular building.
▶ Talk to the children about the Western Wall and the type and size of building which might have originally been on the site. (The Temple was the most holy place for Jewish worship.)
▶ Looking at the photograph of the Jews at the Western Wall, ask the children to discuss the 'clues' which suggest that the men are praying.
▶ Ask the children to consider why visitors to the Western Wall might leave prayers in the cracks of the wall.

Activities
▶ Use these photographs with the map of Israel. Identify the location of Jerusalem.
▶ Ask the children to identify words to describe how Jews might feel praying at the Western Wall.
▶ Invite a Jew who has visited the Western Wall to speak to the children about their experiences.

ISLAM

Muslims praying at home

The photograph shows a Muslim family worshipping Allah in the family home. The father and son are praying in the foreground, the mother and daughter behind them. Everyone has their head covered for worship. Prayer in Islam involves a range of bodily positions, from standing upright; bending forward with hands on the knees; kneeling as shown in the photograph; then prostration with the head touching the prayer mat (a position of complete submission to the will of Allah). Prayer, or salah, five times a day is one of the Five Pillars or requirements of every Muslim.

Discussing the photograph
▶ Discuss with the children what they can see in the photograph.
▶ Talk to the children about the 'clues' which indicate that the family members are praying (such as the kneeling position, the hands in a position of supplication).
▶ Discuss the effect it might have on a person's life to pray five times a day.

Activities
▶ Look at the resources showing Christians and Jews praying and talk about the similarities and differences in the way in which people pray.
▶ Invite a Muslim to explain to the children about the different prayer positions and the prayers that accompany each position. Alternatively, watch a video of Muslims at prayer.
▶ Make a timetable of the five times of day when a Muslim prays: before sunrise, at noon, mid-afternoon, after sunset and in the evening.
▶ Ask the children to sit quietly for about five minutes at noon and at one point during the afternoon to think about someone who is important to them. This will help them to experience the ritual of stopping at specified times for reflection.
▶ Ask the children to talk about the effect that these times of stillness have upon them. What are the benefits?

Video: What a mosque is like, A mosque, Praying in a mosque, Ladies' prayer room

The video shows the exterior and interior of an Islamic mosque and cultural centre. The Muslim symbol of a crescent moon is visible on the dome. Inside the building, the prayer hall has a carpet divided into individual prayer mats.

The photographs show the exterior and interior of a mosque and cultural centre. The mosque has been created within two semi-detached houses. A small sign over the doors indicates that it is a mosque. Inside, the carpet is divided into individual prayer mats. The qibla or direction of Makkah is indicated by a recess in the far wall with a wall hanging displaying a picture of the Ka'bah in Makkah. The Imam can be seen in front leading the men in prayer. The clocks on the wall (to the right of the qibla) show the times of prayer.

The Ladies' prayer room is upstairs and separate from the men. The women are facing towards Makkah, and the carpet is divided into separate prayer mats as in the room below. Both women have their heads covered. (In Orthodox synagogues, women also sit separately from the men, but they usually stay in the same room.)

Discussing the video and photographs
▶ Talk to the children about what they find interesting about these pictures.
▶ Discuss how it must feel to pray in a row close to others who share the same beliefs.
▶ Ask the children to identify the 'clues' that show that this is a Muslim place of worship.

Activities
▶ Visit a mosque to look at the qibla and where men and women worship. In some mosques women will pray behind the men, in a room next door to the men or in a room above.
▶ Compare the mosque visited with the one in the photograph. Ask the children to identify the similarities and differences.

▶ Invite a Muslim to speak to the children about his or her experiences of praying in a large group at the mosque in contrast to the experience of praying at home.

The Ka'bah at Makkah

The photograph shows the Ka'bah at Makkah surrounded by pilgrims from all over the Muslim world performing hajj (or pilgrimage) – a duty that every Muslim should try to undertake once in a lifetime. The Ka'bah is a cube-shaped building in the centre of Makkah. It is covered with a black cloth, beautifully decorated in gold. The cloth is replaced each year.

Embedded in one corner of the Ka'bah is a black stone, which has links with the Prophet Abraham and which the Prophet Muhammad laid at the reconstruction of the Ka'bah. Many thousands of Muslims are shown walking around the Ka'bah in an anticlockwise direction, seven times, as part of the hajj rituals. Before entering Makkah, all pilgrims will leave their day clothes and wear the dress of a pilgrim – two pieces of white cloth (the ihram), a symbol that all appear as equals before Allah.

Discussing the photograph
▶ Talk to the children about special journeys they have made; the purpose of making the journey, how they felt and what they did on arrival. How did they feel when they returned?
▶ Discuss with the children why people visit places of pilgrimage; their possible feelings before leaving and the change it makes to their life on return.
▶ Talk to the children about the number of people they can see in the photograph and the significance of Makkah for Muslims.

Activities
▶ Display this photograph of the Ka'bah with the map of hajj (provided on the CD and linked to Chapter 4: Islam). Ask the children to locate Makkah.
▶ Invite a Muslim who has been on hajj to talk to the children about the experience, including the time spent planning the journey and the cost.
▶ Discuss how the wearing of different clothes can make people feel better or worse than others. How can this situation be addressed?

HINDUISM

Hindu shrine in the home

The photograph shows a family, possibly a grandmother and grandchildren, worshipping together in the family home. They are seated around the family shrine on which is placed pictures and murtis, or images, of gods which are worshipped by the Hindu family. Clearly visible in the centre is a picture and a murti of Lord Krishna. To the left is Ganesh, the elephant-headed god, and to the right a murti of Lord Swaminarayan, a religious teacher respected by many Hindus. The picture on the wall shows Rama, Sita and Lakshmana, whose story is told at Divali. Also on the shrine is a coconut, a smaller murti (possibly of Lord Shiva), a copy of the Bhagavad Gita (a holy book) and a lighted diva. The children's hands are placed together to show respect to God. Hindus will hold their hands in this way when greeting each other with the word, 'Namaste'. Hindus believe that there is a spark of the divine in each of us and it is a way of saying that 'the spark of the divine in me greets the spark of the divine in you'.

Discussing the photograph
▶ Ask the children to talk about the many different objects seen in the picture.
▶ Talk with the children about the 'clues' that suggest that the family is worshipping.

Activities
▶ Invite a Hindu to speak to the children about his or her family shrine and how it is similar or different from that shown in the photograph.
▶ Set up a Hindu shrine in the classroom. (See photocopiable page 60 'A Hindu shrine'.)
▶ Read or listen to a story about one of the gods shown here, such as the story of Lord Ganesh and how he got his elephant head.

Video: What a mandir is like, A mandir, Inside a mandir

The video shows the exterior and interior of a mandir, a Hindu place of worship. Outside, the red flag is a sign that this is a Hindu mandir. Worshippers inside are facing the shrine and singing bhajans, devotional hymns or songs.

The two photographs show the exterior and interior of a mandir. This mandir is dedicated to Lord Krishna and has the 'Aum' symbol beside the name of the mandir and on the red flag. 'Aum' is a sacred word, representing the divine, which Hindus repeat as a mantra. Inside the mandir are three main shrines, with Lord Krishna and Radha in the centre. Lord Krishna is recognisable as he is playing his flute. All the murtis are dressed in fine clothes and jewellery and this is one way in which Hindus show their respect. The murtis are bathed and dressed each morning. To the right can be seen mountains representing the Himalayas.

Discussing the video and photographs

▶ Talk with the children about the different ways in which buildings in the local community are recognisable from symbols shown outside.

▶ Talk with the children about the two symbols that identify this as a Hindu temple or mandir – the 'Aum' and the flag.

▶ Talk about what can be seen inside the mandir. Discuss the ways in which the murtis are shown as important figures for worship. Explain how the murtis are a focal point for the worship of god.

Activities

▶ Look at a map to identify the location of a mandir within the local community.

▶ Visit a mandir to find out about the gods that are particularly worshipped by the local Hindu community. Look at the murtis displayed in the shrine.

▶ Invite a Hindu to talk to the children about their understanding of God and how the images or murtis help a Hindu to worship.

▶ Watch a video/DVD to learn more about how Hindus understand God. For example, *Pathways of Belief: Hinduism* (BBC Education).

Hindus worshipping at the River Ganges

The photograph shows a Hindu priest performing puja or worship on the banks of the River Ganges. The priest (or Brahmin) is wearing the sacred thread which passes over his left shoulder, and he is using marigold flowers as part of the puja. The Ganges is a sacred river for Hindus and many bathe in its waters and perform their morning worship on its banks. Varanasi is one of the Hindu sacred sites on the Ganges; it has around 1,500 temples, palaces, and shrines.

Discussing the photograph

▶ Talk to the children about what can be seen in the photograph and where was taken.

▶ Discuss what might be happening in the foreground of the photograph. Talk about the body postures and the expressions of those involved.

▶ Talk together about the large number of people in the picture – only a few of whom are worshipping. Talk about the reasons why so many might be around the river.

Activities

▶ Locate the route of the River Ganges and the site of Varanasi on the map of India.

▶ Invite a person who has visited India and the Ganges to talk about their experiences and to show their photographs.

▶ Invite a Hindu to speak to the children about the importance of the Ganges to Hindus.

SIKHISM

Video: What a gurdwara is like, A gurdwara, Worship in the gurdwara

The video shows the exterior and interior of a gurdwara – a place of worship for Sikhs. Outside can be seen the Nishan Sahib, the Sikh flag and flagpole. Inside is shown the prayer

hall and the reading of the Guru Granth Sahib, the Sikh holy book.

The two photographs show the exterior and interior of a different gurdwara. On the outside wall is the 'Ik Onkar' symbol. It stands for, 'There is only One God' – the central Sikh belief. Also visible outside is the Nishan Sahib or Sikh flag and flagpole, with the silver Khanda, another Sikh symbol, on the top of the pole.

Inside the gurdwara is shown the holy book the Guru Granth Sahib, resting on a platform under a canopy. The 'Ik Onkar' symbol can be seen on either side of the canopy, while the Khanda is shown in bronze in front of the Guru Granth Sahib and in silver on the front of the offering box. The Khanda consists of the double-edged sword at the centre, the circle of the Kara or bangle and the two Kirpan or swords on either side. The Kara and the Kirpan are two of the 'Five Ks' or symbols worn by Sikhs – the others being the Kesh (uncut hair), the Kangha (comb) and the Kachera (traditional shorts worn as underwear). The Granthi, the reader of the Guru Granth Sahib, is waving a 'chauri' over the scriptures as a mark of respect. The worshipper is bowing before the scriptures as she enters the gurdwara.

Discussing the video and photographs
▶ Talk to the children about what can be seen in the video and in each photograph.
▶ Ask the children to identify the symbols which can be seen both outside and inside the gurdwara.
▶ Discuss the symbols from different religions that are used to identify places of worship.
▶ Discuss how the importance of the Guru Granth Sahib can be seen in the way that it is cared for and displayed.

Activities
▶ Investigate whether there is a gurdwara locally. If there is, find it on a local map.
▶ Visit a gurdwara to learn more about the Sikh symbols and how the Guru Granth Sahib is treated.
▶ Watch a video/DVD, for example, *Pathways of Belief: Sikhism* (BBC Education) to learn more about the Guru Granth Sahib.
▶ Make a model of a gurdwara, showing the large open space for worship in front of the Guru Granth Sahib. Use the picture as a guide for designing the platform on which the holy book rests.

The Golden Temple at Amritsar

The Golden Temple at Amritsar is a holy place for Sikhs. The Temple is set in the middle of a sacred pool, crossed by a causeway. Inside, the Guru Granth Sahib is read continually throughout the day and transmitted by loud speaker. In the evening, following the evening prayers, the Guru Granth Sahib, as in all gurdwaras, is processed along the causeway and is literally 'put to bed' in a separate building. The Guru Granth Sahib is treated as a living Guru or teacher by the Sikhs. Non-Sikhs can visit the Golden Temple and can sit by the lake listening to the reading of the Guru Granth Sahib.

Discussing the photograph
▶ Talk about and compare the different sites (often places of pilgrimage) which are special to different religions.
▶ Ask the children to talk about their feelings and thoughts when they look at the photograph of the Golden Temple.
▶ Discuss the atmosphere of the Temple and its surroundings, from the beauty of the Temple and the bustle of the visitors to the calmness of the water and the coolness of the archways surrounding the lake.

Activities
▶ Display this photograph with the map of India and locate Amritsar.
▶ Invite a person who has visited the Golden Temple to speak to the children about their experience and to show their photographs. If your speaker is a Sikh, invite him or her to speak about the personal effect the visit had.
▶ Listen to a reading of the Guru Granth Sahib either on a CD-Rom or video. Imagine listening to it while sitting by a lake.

BUDDHISM

Buddhist shrine in the home

The photograph shows a Buddhist at his home shrine. The shrine is placed in a quiet corner of his room, on the top of a small chest. A buddharupa, or statue of the Buddha, is at the centre of the shrine with flowers, a symbol of impermanence; incense sticks to perfume the air and a symbol of the sweetness of the Buddha's teaching; and puja bowls which may contain water, rice or fruit. Although a light is not visible here, one is usually present on a shrine. The posture of the man suggests he is paying respect to the Buddha or meditating on the Buddha's teaching.

Discussing the photograph
▶ Ask the children to identify the objects present on the shrine.
▶ Talk to the children about the position of the shrine in a quiet area of the home, and why this might be important.
▶ Discuss what the children think the man is doing and the 'clues' that help them to 'read' the picture.

Activities
▶ Invite a member of the Buddhist community to speak to the children about how he or she follows their beliefs in their home.
▶ Read or listen to a story about the life of the Buddha. (See photocopiable page 76 'Prince Siddhattha – the Buddha'.)
▶ Learn more about the Buddha's teaching from photocopiable page 79 'The Eightfold Path'. Discuss how easy or difficult it would be to follow.

Video: Inside a Buddhist centre

The video shows a meditation room in a large Buddhist centre. The main feature of the room is a statue of the Buddha. He is seated upon and is also holding a lotus flower, which is a special symbol in Buddhism. The Buddha is sitting cross-legged in the lotus position. His right hand is raised and it is believed to be the gesture of the Buddha immediately after he attained enlightenment. (See photocopiable page 78 'Mudras and symbols in Buddhism' for more of the Buddha's hand positions.) Like the Buddha, the meditation room is calm and peaceful.

Discussing the video
▶ Talk about what can be seen in the video.
▶ Look at the statue of Buddha. Explain that he has attained enlightenment. Ask the children how they would express enlightenment.
▶ Ask the children to describe the feeling of the room. How would the room help a person to meditate?

Activities
▶ Find out if there is a Buddhist centre in the local area. Locate it on a local map.
▶ If possible, visit a Buddhist centre. Different groups practise their worship in different ways: some Buddhists chant, while other Buddhists may prefer to meditate in silence.
▶ Invite a member of the Buddhist community to speak to the children about meditation, and practise some techniques together. Ask the children how they feel after they meditate. What do they think might be the benefits of meditation?

Giant Buddha statue

This beautiful statue of the Buddha is in Nepal, situated in the Himalayan Mountains between India and southwest China. There are many large Buddha statues around the world in Buddhist, countries such as Sri Lanka, Burma and Thailand, and both Buddhists and non-Buddhists make special trips to see them. The Buddha is seated in the lotus position on an open lotus flower. In this position, he is firmly balanced. Buddhists aim to achieve

a 'balanced' way of life by following the teaching of the Buddha – the Eightfold Path. The Buddha's face is calm, his eyes lowered in meditation.

Discussing the photograph

▶ Talk to the children about where they like to go and what they do if they want to feel calm and quiet.

▶ Discuss the appearance of the Buddha in the photograph.

▶ Discuss why the artist or sculptor might have wanted to show the Buddha in this way.

Activities

▶ Find out about some of the Buddhist countries shown on the map of the world.

▶ Try to sit quietly in the lotus position. Describe how it feels to sit still.

▶ Challenge the children to create a Buddha using Plasticine or clay. Ask them to think carefully about the position of the body and hands, and the expression on the Buddha's face.

NOTES ON THE PHOTOCOPIABLE PAGES

Word cards   PAGES 18-19

These cards show key words that children will encounter when working on the unit. They include:

▶ words relating to the activities of worship

▶ words to identify sites of religious significance and pilgrimage.

Read through the word cards with the children to familiarise them with the key words of the unit. Ask which words the children have heard before and clarify any they don't understand.

Activities

▶ Cut out the cards and laminate them. Use them as often as possible when talking about ways in which people can belong to a particular religion, group or organisation.

▶ Encourage the children to match the word cards to the pictures in the Resource Gallery.

▶ Use the word cards for displays about 'Worship' and 'Special places'.

▶ Cut out the sacred places word cards and the descriptions. Ask the children to match the cards. Challenge more able children to use the cards as the basis for a guessing game, with one person describing the features of the place and the others guessing the location.

▶ Use the sacred places word cards to label special places of worship on maps.

A place of worship   PAGE 20

The activity sheet provides an opportunity for the children to identify features of a church, synagogue or mosque. The task will develop the children's knowledge about each place of worship. Alternatively it could be used as an assessment task to assess whether the children are able to identify and correctly locate key features of each place. Adapt the ideas on this sheet for other places of worship.

Activities

▶ Enlarge the floor plans or use them as a basis for drawing a large floor map. Cut out the word cards and ask the children to locate the cards in the appropriate places of worship and in the right areas of each building. Try substituting the word cards with pictures, drawn from photographs from the resources.

▶ Use this activity sheet to reinforce learning after watching the videos showing each place of worship, or after discussion of the photographs.

▶ Visit a place of worship and then provide groups of children with this activity sheet. Ask the children to incorporate the work on this sheet into a guidebook of the building to share with other visitors. Alternatively, encourage the children to use the sheet to plan a guided tour of the building.

Worship word cards

pray	**light candles**
worship	**tell sacred stories**
pilgrimage	**remember the past and key people**
reflect	**make offerings**

Sacred places word cards

Bethlehem	**Jesus was born here.**
Nazareth	**Jesus grew up here.**
Jerusalem	**The Dome of the Rock and Western Wall are here.**
Makkah	**Muslims should visit here once in a lifetime.**
Amritsar	**The Golden Temple is here.**
River Ganges	**The sacred river for Hindus.**

A place of worship

- Cut out the word cards and group them together into 'Things you would find in a church'; 'Things you would find in a synagogue', and 'Things you would find in a mosque'. Some things may be found in more than one place of worship.

- Use the floorplans below, or copy one onto a big sheet of paper, and label the things you would find in a place of worship.

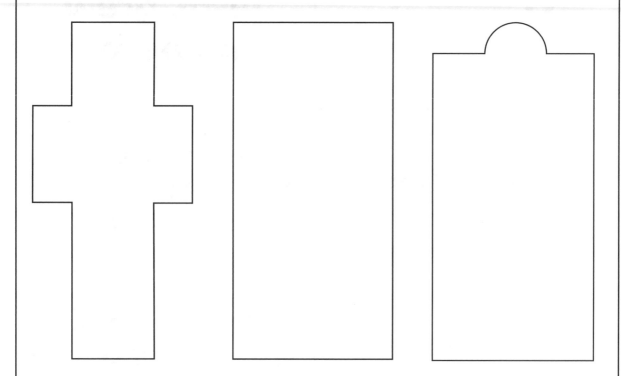

altar	baptismal font	cloakroom
pews	Ark	qiblah (direction of Makkah)
choir	Torah scrolls	clocks
nave	bimah (reading desk)	prayer mats
lectern	ner tamid (the everlasting light)	washroom
pulpit	menorah	shoe racks

CHRISTIANITY

Content and skills

This chapter addresses the questions: 'What do we know from the Bible about the events in Jesus' life?' and 'Why is Jesus important to Christians today?'. The focus of this chapter is to enable Key Stage 2 children to develop a coherent picture of the life of Jesus as told in the Gospels and as interpreted by artists. It is designed to build on the knowledge of Christian festivals and the stories about Jesus gained at Key Stage 1 and prepare for further study of the teachings of Jesus at Key Stage 3. The unit requires children to engage with the biblical stories through use of Children's Bibles, to reflect on the images portrayed in art and to discuss with Christians the impact of these stories on their lives.

The study of Jesus, his life and his teaching is a key focus for teaching and learning in religious education in all LEA Agreed Syllabuses. It is reflected in the themes identified in the non-statutory framework for RE; specifically the themes of 'beliefs and questions', 'teaching and authority' and 'inspirational people'. Through this chapter the children will develop their skills of analysis and interpretation; they will develop their religious vocabulary and their understanding of the use of a range of sources and they will also be able to describe the impact of Jesus on people at the time, and Christians today.

The Resource Gallery for 'Christianity' on the CD, together with the teachers' notes and photocopiable pages in this chapter, support teaching and learning about the life of Jesus. The teachers' notes contain background information about the resources and include ways of using them as a whole class, for group work or as individuals.

Some of the activities link with other areas of the curriculum, such as literacy and art and design. Wherever possible, the activities encourage the children to ask questions and develop an enquiring approach to their learning.

Resources on the CD-ROM

The resources comprise a range of paintings portraying the life of Jesus. There are also video clips of Christians explaining why Christmas and Easter are important festivals for them as believers. These resources serve to develop the children's understanding of the life of Jesus and his impact on others.

Photocopiable pages

The photocopiable pages in the book are also provided in PDF format on the CD-ROM and can be printed from there. They include:
- ▶ word cards containing essential vocabulary for the unit
- ▶ an activity sheet that explores what people can learn from Jesus' teachings
- ▶ an activity sheet that explores the concept of how Jesus changed people's lives
- ▶ an activity sheet based on the last week of Jesus' life.

NOTES ON THE CD-ROM RESOURCES

A picture of Jesus, A mosaic of Christ Pantocrator

The photographs show two images of Jesus, the first a painting; the second a 12th-century mosaic of Christ Pantocrator, Christ, 'the Ruler of all'.

There are similarities between the two images – in each picture Jesus is depicted with a halo and his right hand is giving a blessing. There are also differences – in the mosaic Jesus is wearing more ornate robes and is holding the Gospels. The placing of the mosaic in the apse (the curved part of the roof of the basilica) represents the power and importance of the figure.

Discussing the pictures
▶ Ask the children to talk about who and what is seen in each picture.
▶ Talk to the children about the similarities and differences between the two images.
▶ Discuss the kind of figure represented by each image and the feelings that each image evokes in the viewer. Which do the children prefer and why?

Activities
▶ Use the images as inspiration for observational drawings or for designing individual mosaics.
▶ Read some stories about Jesus and compare the images of Jesus in these stories with the images portrayed in the two pictures. Suggested extracts: Luke 23:3–4: (Jesus as king); Luke 19:7–10: (mixing with sinners); Luke 20:20–26: (clever at arguing); Mark 11:15–19 (Jesus is angry, and his teaching captivates the people).

Jesus' baptism

This stained glass window depicts Jesus' baptism by John the Baptist. The story is told in Matthew 3:1–6 and 3:13–17. John, wearing a rough coat of camel hair, was preaching that people should repent for their sins and was baptising them in the River Jordan. John recognised Jesus' importance and suggested that Jesus should baptise him, but Jesus asks for John to be the baptist. At the moment of baptism, the gospel says that the Spirit of God descended on Jesus like a dove, although this episode is not shown in the window.

Discussing the picture
▶ Talk about the characters and the actions taking place in the picture.
▶ Discuss the symbolism seen in the window: the halos, the water, the position of Jesus' hands and the purple robe (which the figure on the left is waiting to put over Jesus).
▶ Discuss the similarities between Jesus' baptism and adult baptism.

Activities
▶ Read the extracts from St Matthew's Gospel on which these events are based.
▶ Discuss how the artist's portrayal of John the Baptist matches the Gospel account.
▶ Talk to the children about how the Gospels describe what happened after the baptism. Matthew says: 'At that moment heaven opened; he saw the Spirit of God descending like a dove to alight upon him,' (New English Bible, Matthew 3:16). Discuss what Christians might understand by these words and how some artists have portrayed the words visually, either as a dove or a beam of light.
▶ Give each group a copy of the stained glass window backed on sugar paper and ask them to decide how they might portray the links between God and Jesus at the moment of baptism, and to illustrate their ideas.

Jesus in the temple at 12 years old

The painting by William Holman Hunt shows Jesus in the Temple in Jerusalem when he was 12 years old. The story is told in Luke 2:41–52. Jesus' parents take him to Jerusalem for the festival of Passover. When his parents are on the journey home, they discover that Jesus is missing and find him in the Temple in discussion with the teachers who are amazed at his intelligence. Jesus says to his parents, 'Did you not know I was bound to be in my Father's house?' The picture shows Mary with Jesus and to the left are the teachers or rabbis wearing prayer shawls, with one of the rabbis holding the Torah scrolls.

Discussing the picture
▶ Talk about the different characters in the picture – in particular the contrasting ages of Jesus and the rabbis.
▶ Discuss the significance of writing verse 49 from Luke 2 around the painting.
▶ Discuss what the children might learn about Jesus simply by looking at this painting; for example, Jesus' relationship with his mother and with the rabbis; the location of the event.

Activities
▶ Retell the story of the visit to the Temple by Jesus, Mary and Joseph.

▶ Print and mount a copy of the painting for each group in the class. Overlay a sheet of paper with a window cut in it to isolate sections of the painting; for example one group might see only Jesus and his mother, another group might see only the rabbis with the Torah. In groups, ask the children to describe what is visible and to imagine the conversation or thoughts of the characters. Come together as a class to discuss the ideas.

▶ Discuss what the artist is trying to say about Jesus and how Christians might understand the message of this painting.

Temptations of Christ

The painting shows the devil tempting Jesus during the 40 days that he spent in the wilderness before beginning his teaching. The story is told in Luke 4:1–13. The devil tried to tempt Jesus three times: first to change stones into bread; second to rule all the kingdoms of the world in exchange for worshipping the devil; and third to test God by throwing himself from the parapet, or pinnacle of the temple. The Temptations are about the use and misuse of power in both personal and public life. Analogies for children begin with issues of stealing and disobedience.

Discussing the picture

▶ Talk to the children about the meaning of the word 'temptation'.

▶ Discuss the two figures shown in the painting and the relationship between them (indicated by the position of their bodies).

▶ Ask the children to think about the 'power' of the figures and who appears the most powerful in the painting.

Activities

▶ Read or tell the story of the temptations of Jesus from Luke 4:1–13.

▶ Focus on the figure of the devil and the stone and the bread he is holding. Ask the children to write speech bubbles paraphrasing the way he tries to persuade Jesus.

▶ Make a mind map of the reasons why, and the circumstances when, it would be tempting to change stones into bread. There could be good and bad reasons.

▶ Brainstorm temptations which affect the children and choose one to complete the mind map exercise above; thinking of good and bad reasons for giving in to this temptation.

▶ Role-play one or more of the temptation scenarios in pairs.

▶ Re-create the painting with the devil presenting the second or third temptations: think of the visual image, the speech bubbles of persuasion and Jesus' response.

▶ Invite a Christian to share their perspective on the painting with the children, explaining how it develops their understanding of Jesus.

Jesus overturns the moneychangers' tables

The painting shows the chaos in the surrounds of the temple as Jesus drives out the moneychangers, the story told in Luke 19:45–46. The scene includes traders of fruit and flat bread and those selling animals for sacrifice in the temple. Animal sacrifice was a practice at that time and Mary and Joseph had made an offering of two turtle doves or pigeons when Jesus was presented in the temple as a baby (Luke 2:22–24). Jesus was objecting to those who were not honest and over-charged, exploiting the pilgrims.

Discussing the picture

▶ Talk about the different types of people represented in the painting.

▶ Distinguish between the characters who are being driven out of the temple and those who are simply moving away from the commotion.

▶ Discuss the issues underlying the event; for example, fairness in charging others, and not exploiting those who have no choice.

Activities

▶ Remind the children about the characters who were being driven out and the reasons why. Ask the children to think of titles or captions for the picture.

▶ Discuss with the children what we can learn about Jesus' character from the events depicted in the painting.

▶ Write a newspaper report of the event from the point of view of one of the traders, explaining why the moneychangers were driven out and how this made Jesus unpopular with the moneychangers and the religious leaders in the temple.

Last Supper

The painting shows Jesus and his disciples at the Last Supper or Passover Meal. The story is told in Luke 22:1–34. The Passover Meal, still celebrated today as the Seder Meal, is a time for Jews to commemorate how their ancestors fled slavery in Egypt to freedom in the Promised Land. It is a solemn, yet joyous occasion.

This is the meal when Jesus tells the disciples to share the wine together and compares the blessed bread with his own body, a ritual which remains important to Christians today. However, at the time of the Last Supper, Judas has already betrayed Jesus, and before the end of the meal Peter is told that he will deny knowing Jesus before daybreak. Luke also tells of an argument between the disciples as to who was the most important. These themes of betrayal and dispute about importance can be explored at Key Stage 2.

Discussing the picture
▶ Ask the children to talk about the way in which the characters are relating to each other, either by looking at each other or by physically touching each other.
▶ Discuss the feelings portrayed by the artist; for example, whether it is a happy or comfortable scene between all of the characters.

Activities
▶ Read or retell the story of the Last Supper from a children's Bible, Luke 22:1–34.
▶ Explore the different types of betrayal of Jesus by Judas and Peter. Discuss with the children why each of the characters might have acted in this way and whether Peter was a wholly bad person or just scared. 'Hot seat' each character to explore the issues further.
▶ Discuss with the children how, at particular points, the story might have been different if the characters had acted differently.
▶ Identify and discuss times when the children feel they have been betrayed. Discuss what can be done to put the situation right.
▶ Visit a church and ask the vicar or priest to explain how his or her church commemorates the Last Supper during Holy Week. How do Christians today celebrate the Last Supper during weekly services?

Crucifixion

The painting shows the crucifixion of Jesus with two criminals. One of the soldiers is offering Jesus a sponge containing wine and in the foreground soldiers are throwing dice for Jesus' clothes. Nailed to the cross above Jesus' head is an inscription reading: 'This is the king of the Jews'. The painting is medieval and therefore the clothes and style are of that period.

Discussing the picture
▶ Talk with the children about the scene and characters depicted in the painting.
▶ Discuss the way in which the different characters are reacting to the crucifixion.
▶ Discuss the way Christians might feel when looking at this painting.

Activities
▶ Divide the painting into sections and focus on the responses of the different characters. Ask the children to create thought and speech bubbles around the painting expressing the different thoughts and feelings.
▶ Visit a church to look at the Stations of the Cross (pictures that mark the journey of Jesus to the cross).
▶ Look at the words of some of the hymns or songs which are sung in churches on Good Friday, such as 'Bitter was the night' by Sidney Carter.

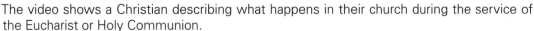

Video: The Eucharist

The video shows a Christian describing what happens in their church during the service of the Eucharist or Holy Communion.

Discussing the video

▶ Talk to the children about the times when they share a meal with their family or friends and their feelings associated with these events.
▶ Talk to the children about the reasons why Christians eat bread and drink wine together.

Activities

▶ Look at the painting of Jesus' Last Supper with his disciples and make links between this and the Holy Communion shared in churches today.
▶ Invite a Christian to talk about what it means to them to celebrate Holy Communion.

Empty cross, Easter garden

The empty cross is a symbol of resurrection and therefore of hope for Christians today.

The Easter Garden commemorates the story of the women visiting the tomb on Easter Day to put spices on Jesus' body and finding that Jesus' body had gone. The gravel path leads away from the tomb. The story is told in different ways in each of the Gospels. Luke's Gospel (Luke 23:55– 24;11) tells of two men, presumably angels, asking why the women are looking among the dead for the living – the message of the resurrection.

Discussing the pictures

▶ Ask the children to reflect on the picture of the Easter Garden and whether it looks like a garden of sadness or joy.
▶ Discuss the symbolism of the Easter Garden and the empty cross.

Activities

▶ Read the story from Luke's Gospel of the women visiting the tomb to anoint the body.
▶ Create caption cards to retell the story of the Sunday morning when the women found the empty tomb. Attach the cards to the picture of the Easter Garden.
▶ Design Easter cards with an Easter garden or a cross. Include an appropriate statement from one of the gospels inside the card.
▶ Make Good Friday and Easter Day displays, including symbols such as a crucifix, hot-cross buns and dice for Good Friday, and an Easter garden, empty cross and Easter eggs for Easter Day.

Video: Why Christmas is special, Video: Why Easter is special

These video clips show Christians explaining why the festivals of Christmas and Easter are celebrated, and how they themselves celebrate the festivals in their place of worship and in their homes.

Discussing the videos

▶ Talk to the children about their awareness of the festivals of Christmas and Easter, whether it is through the giving of presents and Easter eggs or through attending church services.
▶ Discuss the events described on the videos and the ways in which the festivals are celebrated in the place of worship and in the home.
▶ Talk with the children about the events described on the video which they might also celebrate in their homes – whether or not they are from a Christian family.

Activities

▶ Write about how the Christians shown in the videos celebrate the festivals of Christmas and Easter. Draw pictures of them and display them on a 'Festivals' board.
▶ Interview Christians and ask them to describe the way they celebrate the major Christian festivals. Compare the similarities and differences in the ways they celebrate. Take photographs of the people interviewed and display them with their responses.

NOTES ON THE PHOTOCOPIABLE PAGES

Christianity word cards

PAGE 27-28

These cards show key words that relate to Jesus' life. Read through the word cards with the children to familiarise them with the key words of the unit. Ask which words the children have heard before and clarify any they don't understand.

Activities
▶ Cut out the cards and laminate them. Use them as often as possible when talking about ways in which people can belong to a particular religion, group or organisation.
▶ Encourage the children to match the word cards to the pictures in the Resource Gallery.
▶ Use the word cards for displays about 'Jesus' or the 'Festival of Easter'.

Jesus the teacher

PAGES 29

The activity sheet contains a collection of sayings of Jesus from the New Testament. They are all related to how followers of Jesus should live their lives. They therefore relate to the impact of Jesus' teachings on Christians today.

Activities
▶ Cut up the separate statements. Give each group one statement and ask them to discuss what it means and how they would put it into action.
▶ Ask each group to role-play their responses to the rest of the class.
▶ Discuss which might be the easiest and most difficult sayings to live by.

Jesus changed lives

PAGE 30

This sheet considers two examples of how Jesus changed the lives of people he encountered and constructs 'two case studies' of how the life and teaching of Jesus changes people's lives today.

James was a fishermen recruited to be a disciple as he fished by the Sea of Galilee, 'Sarah' witnessed how a crowd of five thousand were fed from five loaves and two fish. The story is told in Luke 9:10–17. Christians describe this event in different ways: some say it is a parable signifying the sharing of God's word; some say it is a miracle of multiplication – that this small amount of food did feed a large number; others say it was a miracle of sharing – that, given the example of sharing this small amount of food rather than keeping it for oneself, others were prompted to share their own supplies. Discuss these different interpretations with the children.

Activities
▶ Make links between the 'case studies' on the activity sheet and the biblical stories.
▶ Use the model of these case studies for the children to develop a further case study about a well-known Christian, such as Mother Teresa, Martin Luther King or Elizabeth Fry.
▶ Develop a case study about a Christian today. For example, the children could interview a member of the local Church community, a Christian friend or member of their family.

Jesus' last week

PAGE 31

This activity sheet shows the last week in Jesus' life and includes questions for the children to reflect on. The questions are designed to engage the children more deeply with the story and in some instances to relate the actions and feelings to their own experiences.

Activities
▶ Cut the activity sheet into separate pictures with their captions and questions. Ask each group of children to discuss one of the separate pictures and share their responses.
▶ Use each illustration and caption as the basis for writing newspaper accounts.
▶ Link the illustrations and captions with the paintings shown in the resource gallery. Make a display of the paintings, illustrations and the children's writing.

Jesus

disciples

John baptises Jesus

Jesus visits the Temple

Jesus becomes angry with the traders

Jesus' temptations

Last Supper

a disciple betrays Jesus

crucifixion

resurrection

the Garden Tomb

Jesus the teacher

- Discuss and explain the meanings of some of these sayings by Jesus.

1. I was hungry, and you fed me. I was thirsty, and you gave me a drink.

_____

_____

_____

2. Love your neighbour as yourself.

_____

_____

_____

3. Blessed are the peacemakers.

_____

_____

_____

4. It is easier for a camel to go through the eye of a needle, than for a rich man to enter into the kingdom of God.

_____

_____

_____

Illustration © Sarah Warburton

Jesus changed lives

James

- He was a fisherman.

- He lived and worked by the Sea of Galilee.

- Jesus asked James to follow him. James spent the rest of his life travelling and teaching with Jesus.

Sarah

- She lived in Bethsaida and went to hear Jesus speak on a hill near the Sea of Galilee.

- She watched a boy produce five loaves and two fish, and saw everyone share food together.

- Sarah learned that sharing together was important.

Write a profile of someone whose life has been inspired by Jesus. You could imagine someone who went to hear Jesus speak or talk to someone in your local community.

■ SCHOLASTIC
PHOTOCOPIABLE

Jesus' last week

Jesus arrives in Jerusalem. What did the onlookers feel on this day?

Jesus overthrows the moneychangers' tables. Why do you think he did that?

Jesus holds his last supper with his disciples.
Did they know it would be their last supper with him?

Judas betrays Jesus. How would you feel if you were betrayed?

Peter says that he does not know Jesus.
Why do you think Peter did this?

Jesus was crucified on the cross.
How did the onlookers and disciples feel on this day?

Illustrations © Sarah Warburton

JUDAISM

Content and skills

This chapter focuses on the question, 'What is the Torah and why is it important to Jews?'. It addresses the question by considering the impact of the Torah on Jewish daily life, festivals, and celebrations of rites of passage, specifically Bar and Bat Mitzvah.

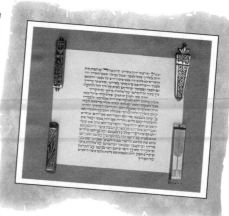

The study of sacred texts, their origins, teachings and authority, and their use in individual and communal worship is a key area for teaching in religious education in most LEA Agreed Syllabuses for RE. The study of sacred texts also features as a theme in the non-statutory framework for religious education.

At Key Stage 2, children can develop their religious vocabulary by discussing the meanings of beliefs and teachings found in sacred texts; they can describe the impact of these on believers and can reflect on whether these texts have messages which can apply more widely and even to their own lives. The discussion areas and activities can be adapted to suit a study of the Bible, Qur'an or the Guru Granth Sahib.

The Resource Gallery on the CD-ROM, together with the teachers' notes and photocopiable pages in this chapter, support teaching and learning about the Torah. The teachers' notes contain background information about the resources and include ways of using them as a whole class, for group work or as individuals. Some of the activities link with other areas of the curriculum, such as literacy and art. Wherever possible, the activities encourage the children to ask questions and develop an enquiring approach to their learning.

Resources on the CD-ROM

The resources include video footage of the Torah being read in the synagogue and an audio extract of the reading of the Shema in Hebrew and English. There are also photographs illustrating the use of sacred text in the mezuzah, the celebration of Bar and Bat Mitzvah and Simchat Torah. These resources serve to develop children's understanding of religion in the home and place of worship and what it means to belong to a religion.

Photocopiable pages

The photocopiable pages in the book are also provided in PDF format on the CD-ROM and can be printed from there. They include:
▶ word cards containing essential vocabulary for the unit
▶ an activity sheet showing the words of the Shema
▶ an activity sheet that explores the concept of kosher
▶ an activity sheet on guidelines for living through the Ten Commandments.

NOTES ON THE CD-ROM RESOURCES

Video: Using the Torah in the synagogue

The video shows how the Sefer Torah (the Torah scroll) is used during a synagogue service. The Torah scrolls are kept in the Ark, a special cupboard. In a purpose-built synagogue, the Ark faces towards the Western Wall in Jerusalem. The scrolls are kept in a decorated velvet or silk covering with a silver breastplate hanging over the cover. The top of the scroll is covered by silver casings with bells. Before the Torah is read, the Rabbi and a member of the congregation read a blessing from the prayer book in Hebrew. The Rabbi reads from the Torah, using a 'yad' (or pointer) to point to the words. The 'yad' is used to prevent smudging of the hand-written scrolls. After the reading, the Torah scroll is raised so that the whole congregation can witness that the words came from the Torah, the 'teaching' for the Jewish people. The Torah scroll is then rewound and 'dressed' again in the coverings before being replaced in the Ark.

The video takes place in a Reform synagogue, as Orthodox Jews do not have or recognise women rabbis.

Discussing the video
▶ Before watching the video, discuss how the children might look after a book or something that was precious to them.
▶ After watching the video, discuss how the children could tell that the Torah was extremely precious to the Jewish people.
▶ Talk about why holy books are special to religious communities.

Activities
▶ Visit a synagogue to look at the Sefer Torah and learn how difficult it is to read Hebrew.
▶ Read a story which is found in the Torah, for example, the story of Moses leading the slaves to freedom, and discuss why this is important to the Jewish people.
▶ Read and discuss the Ten Commandments (see photocopiable page 40) to learn about some of the laws that are important to Jews.
▶ Invite a Rabbi to speak about why the Torah is so important to the Jewish community, about the significance of the blessings before the Torah is read and how the Torah guides Jews in life.

Mezuzah cases and mezuzah scroll, Audio: The Shema

The mezuzah scroll is made from parchment and on it is the Shema, the most important statement of belief for Jews. It is from the Torah, Deuteronomy 6:4–9, and begins 'Hear O Israel; the Lord thy God is One'. The scroll is handwritten in Hebrew, rolled, placed in a mezuzah case and nailed to the front doorpost of a Jewish home and to internal doorposts, excepting the bathroom. Mezuzah cases vary in design and in the materials used, but most will have the Hebrew letter 'shin', which is the first letter of the Hebrew word 'Shaddai', one of the names for God. The mezuzah reminds the people living there, and visitors, of their Jewish beliefs. On entering the house, many will touch the mezuzah.

In the audio resource, the Shema is read first in Hebrew, and then in English. The Shema is repeated by all Jews during the weekly Shabbat services held in the synagogue. Its recitation reminds all Jews of their belief in One God and the commandment to love God with all their heart, to teach their children about God, and to remember God at all times of the day. The commandment to write the statement 'the Lord thy God is One' is fulfilled by having a mezuzah on the doorpost of the home.

Discussing the photograph and audio clip
▶ Discuss how a visitor might learn what is important to a family by the objects they have in their home.
▶ Discuss the effect that having a mezuzah on the front doorpost might have on a Jewish family of children and adults.

Activities
▶ Use the translation of the Shema on photocopiable page 39 while listening to the audio clip.
▶ Invite a Jew to speak to the children about the meaning of the opening of the Shema, 'Hear O Israel, the Lord thy God is One'.
▶ Discuss the power or authority of written words to guide people in their lives.
▶ Using the translation of the Shema (photocopiable page 39), ask the children, working in groups, to highlight the commandments given. Make links between the statement 'write them on your doorposts' and the mezuzah. The statement 'they shall be like frontlets between your eyes' refers to the use of tefillin, small leather boxes containing scrolls like those in the mezuzah case, which are strapped to the forehead and the arms of male Jews for weekday prayers. These are also ways of reminding a Jew of the commandments in the Shema. Discuss how Jewish parents teach the commandments to their children.

▶ Ask the children to think of their own guidelines for living. Write the children's ideas on a large piece of paper and decide together where to place them as a reminder.

Kosher foods

The picture shows a collection of kosher food products. The term 'kosher' refers to food or objects that are ritually fit for consumption or use, according to Jewish law. The dietary laws are set out in the book of Deuteronomy, which states that animals with a cloven hoof and which chew the cud (sheep and goats) are kosher, but not the pig which has a cloven hoof but does not chew the cud. Fish with fins and scales are kosher, but shellfish are not. Meat and milk cannot be mixed, either in the same meal or in the kitchen, so Jewish families will have two sets of utensils kept completely separate from each other (one set for meat and one set for milk products). Manufactured food products, such as those shown, have a special stamp on the packet stating that it is kosher.

Discussing the photograph
▶ Discuss how some people do not eat certain foods for religious or ethical reasons.
▶ Ask the children which food products they recognise.
▶ Discuss the use of Hebrew writing and the kosher symbol (sometimes two letters in a circle as top left on the couscous box).

Activities
▶ Ask a Jewish parent or helper to speak to the children about how they organise their menus and kitchen in order to keep the kosher laws.
▶ Ask the children to spot the kosher symbol on food products in their local supermarket.
▶ Make a collection of kosher products for display in the classroom.
▶ Identify kosher and non-kosher products using photocopiable page 41.
▶ Plan a menu for a small kosher party. Remember that ham, pork pies and sausage rolls cannot be included.
▶ Discuss the positive aspects of coming from a kosher home and the difficulties of keeping kosher for some children with non-Jewish friends.

Bar Mitzvah, Bat Mitzvah

These photographs show a boy and girl preparing for their Bar and Bat Mitzvah, respectively. 'Bar Mitzvah' means 'Son of the Commandment' and 'Bat Mitzvah' – 'Daughter of the Commandment'. The boy's ceremony takes place at thirteen years of age, the girl's at twelve years of age. The form of the ceremony is different in different communities.

The photographs show both children preparing the portion, or section, of the Torah which they will read in the synagogue. The boy is wearing his prayer shawl and capel, and on the bimah (the reading desk on which the Torah scroll is placed), there is also a card with the blessings which are read before the Torah reading. Reading from the Torah is very difficult as the Hebrew does not contain vowels, so the reader has to practise for many months before the ceremony. Becoming Bar or Bat Mitzvah is very important as it marks the time when the boy or girl is regarded as an adult in religious terms. They may then take a more active role in the synagogue. These photographs have been taken in Reform synagogues as Orthodox Jews do not have or recognise women rabbis.

Discussing the photographs
▶ Talk with the children about the ages and events which will make them feel grown up.
▶ Discuss whether the children feel that thirteen and twelve are the right ages to start taking on some of the responsibilities of an adult.
▶ Discuss how the people, special clothes and the reading of the Torah indicate that this is a special event.

Activities
▶ Make a list together of some of the responsibilities that can be undertaken by thirteen and twelve year olds.
▶ Invite someone who can read Hebrew to help the children to read one or two simple words.

▶ Invite a young Jewish person who has celebrated their Bar or Bat Mitzvah to talk to the children about the ceremony, how they prepared for it and how they felt when reading the Torah in front of everyone in the synagogue.

Simchat Torah, Celebrating Simchat Torah

The festival of Simchat Torah is celebrated in September or October each year and marks the end of one cycle of reading the Torah and the beginning of the next cycle. Each week in the synagogue a portion of the Torah is read so that the whole Torah is read during the year. At Simchat Torah, the end of the book of Deuteronomy, the account of the death of Moses is read. However, the Torah cannot be left 'unread' until the next week, so on the same day, the opening chapter of Genesis, the story of creation is read.

In 'Celebrating Simchat Torah', in this particular synagogue, the scroll has been opened to allow this to happen. However, in most synagogues, two scrolls will be used, one for the reading in Deuteronomy, the other for Genesis. Simchat Torah, also referred to as 'Rejoicing in the Law', is a joyful occasion. There is a tradition of processing, and even dancing, with the scrolls seven times around the synagogue; paper flags are waved by the children.

Discussing the photographs
▶ Discuss how the importance, or 'authority', of the Torah means that the cycle of reading it is marked with a special festival.
▶ Talk about the reasons for other festivals, both in Judaism and in other religions.

Activities
▶ Copy the end verses of Deuteronomy and the opening verses of Genesis onto separate sheets of 'parchment' in the form of a scroll. Invite two children to read the verses to the rest of the class.
▶ Make some paper Simchat Torah flags. These are rectangular pieces of paper attached to a stick and decorated with Jewish symbols such as pictures of the Torah scrolls or the Star of David.

Celebrating Shavuot

Shavuot is celebrated in May/June. The festival is also called 'The Season of the Giving of Our Torah' for it commemorates the time when all the Israelites assembled at Mount Sinai and Moses brought God's Ten Sayings or Commandments to the Jewish people. Shavuot is also a harvest festival when the first fruits are brought in. Some communities decorate their homes and synagogues with flowers.

This photograph shows symbolic items on the table. Fresh flowers are a reminder that Shavuot is a harvest festival. The following are symbols of the Torah: water quenches a person's thirst; wine makes people feel glad; oil causes a person's face to shine as does the study of the Torah; honey is sweet like the Torah; milk feeds the body; and light from the candles 'lightens' the eyes in the sense of 'enlightenment'. Also on the table is a cheesecake and cheese straws; it is traditional on Shavuot to eat foods made from milk. The challah, red wine and candles are normally on the table for most Jewish festivals.

Discussing the photograph
▶ Talk about the importance of the Torah for Jews and remind the children of the festival of Simchat Torah which celebrated the end of the cycle of reading.
▶ Discuss the symbolism of the water, wine, oil, honey and milk, and the children's associations with some of the items on the table.

Activities
▶ Read Exodus 19 and 20 from a children's Bible.
▶ Role-play when Moses brings the Ten Commandments down from Mount Sinai. Discuss and debate the meaning of the Ten Commandments through individual 'characters' challenging Moses about the meaning of each one.
▶ Divide the Commandments into those about the worship of God and those related to behaviour towards others. Write each group on 'Torah' scrolls.
▶ Invite a Jew to speak about the celebration of Shavuot in their synagogue.

NOTES ON THE PHOTOCOPIABLE PAGES

Judaism word cards
PAGES 37-38

These cards show key words that children will encounter when working on the unit:
▶ words relating to symbols of Judaism in the home and synagogue
▶ words to describe festivals and celebrations.
Read through the word cards with the children to familiarise them with the key words of the unit. Clarify any words that the children don't understand.

Activities
▶ Cut out the cards and laminate them. Encourage the children to match the word cards to the pictures in the Resource Gallery.
▶ Use the word cards for displays about the role of the Torah for festivals and celebrations.

The Shema
PAGE 39

The Shema is a Jewish prayer that is repeated during each service in the synagogue. It is written on the mezuzah scroll. It is important because it is a statement of Jewish belief in the One God and a commandment to proclaim the Oneness of God at all times of the day and through one's actions.

Activities
▶ Using the activity sheet, highlight all the things Jews are commanded to do.
▶ Listen to the reading of the Shema on the audio resource.
▶ Discuss the meaning/s of 'the Lord is One'.

The Ten Commandments
PAGE 40

The Ten Sayings or Commandments can be found in the Christian Bible, Exodus 20. Of the ten, the first four commandments are to do with the worship of God and the remaining six are guidelines for daily life. They were given by God to the Jewish people through Moses and were given at a time when the Jews were becoming a community. Ask the children to consider whether these commandments are important for communities today.

Activities
▶ Cut up the sheet of commandments into ten separate strips. Ask the children in groups to select the three commandments which they feel are the most important. Compare and discuss the different responses.
▶ Discuss which of these commandments would be most difficult to keep in today's society.
▶ Use this activity sheet in conjunction with activities on the festival of Shavuot. Role-play the scene when Moses presents the commandments to the people.

Are these foods kosher?
PAGE 41

For Jews, the food laws for what is kosher are found in scripture, one reference being Deuteronomy 14. No shellfish can be eaten, meat and milk or milk products cannot be prepared using the same cooking utensils and cannot be eaten at the same meal, and no pork products can be eaten. The food items illustrated include kosher (chicken soup, milk and cheese), non-kosher (bacon and eggs) and a bowl of fruit which is neither kosher nor non-kosher.

Activities
▶ Ask the children to circle those food items on the activity sheet that are non-kosher and therefore could not be eaten by Jews.
▶ For further activities, see above notes for the photograph 'Kosher foods'.

Judaism word cards (1)

Jew

Sefer Torah

mezuzah

Shema

kosher

Bar Mitzvah

Bat Mitzvah

Simchat Torah

Shavuot

Moses

the Ten Commandments

The Shema

*Hear, O Israel, the Eternal One is our God, the
Eternal God is One.
Praise forever be God's majesty.
And you shall love the Eternal One your God
with all your heart, with all your soul and with
all your might.
Let these words, which I command you this day,
be always in your heart.
Teach them diligently to your children; speak of
them in your home, and on your way, when you
lie down and when you rise up.
Bind them as a sign upon your hand, let them be
like frontlets between your eyes.
Inscribe them on the doorposts of your house
and on your gates.*

Deuteronomy 6:4-9

Illustration © Sarah Warburton

The Ten Commandments

1. YOU SHALL HAVE ONLY ONE GOD.

2. YOU SHALL NOT MAKE FOR YOURSELF ANY IDOL, NOR BOW DOWN TO IT OR WORSHIP IT.

3. YOU SHALL NOT MISUSE THE NAME OF THE LORD YOUR GOD.

4. YOU SHALL REMEMBER AND KEEP THE SABBATH DAY HOLY.

5. RESPECT YOUR FATHER AND MOTHER.

6. YOU MUST NOT KILL.

7. YOU MUST NOT BE UNFAITHFUL.

8. YOU MUST NOT STEAL.

9. YOU MUST NOT TELL LIES AGAINST YOUR NEIGHBOUR.

10. YOU MUST NOT BE JEALOUS OF ANYTHING THAT BELONGS TO YOUR NEIGHBOUR.

Illustration © Sarah Warburton

Are these foods kosher?

- Circle the foods that are not kosher.

Chicken soup

Eggs and soldiers

Crabs and lobsters

Steak and chips

Bacon and eggs

Milk and cheese

Fish on a platter

Bowl of fruit

Cheeseburger

Cheesy omelette

- Complete the sentence:

These foods are not kosher because…

_____

_____

_____

_____

SCHOLASTIC
PHOTOCOPIABLE

ISLAM

Content and skills

This chapter addresses the questions, 'What does it mean to be a Muslim?' and 'How do Muslims express their beliefs in practice?'. There is a focus on the key beliefs of Islam – specifically, belief in one God, Allah; belief in Muhammad as the Prophet or Messenger of Allah; and belief in the Qur'an as the revealed Word of Allah. The ideas in the chapter then address how a Muslim translates those beliefs into actions through following the Five Pillars of Islam: the Shahadah – profession of faith; Salah – prayer five times a day; Zakat – the regular giving of money to the poor and needy in the community; Sawm – fasting during the month of Ramadan; and Hajj – pilgrimage to Makkah. This chapter links closely to Chapter 1 'Places of worship' and develops the meaning of 'worship' in Islam.

Muslim beliefs and practices are key areas for teaching and learning at Key Stage 2 in all LEA Agreed Syllabuses for religious education and are reflected in the themes of 'teaching and authority' and 'symbols and religious expression' in the non-statutory framework for religious education. A study of the resources in this chapter should enable Key Stage 2 children to develop their religious vocabulary to explain the impact of beliefs on individuals and communities; to explain how religious sources are used to provide answers to ethical issues; and to discuss ways in which Muslims show they belong to a community, relating this to their own experience.

The Resource Gallery for 'Islam' on the CD-ROM, together with the teachers' notes and photocopiable pages in this chapter, support teaching and learning about worship in Islam. The teachers' notes contain background information about the resources and include ways of using them as a whole class, for group work or as individuals. Some of the activities link with other areas of the curriculum, such as literacy. Wherever possible, the activities encourage the children to ask questions and develop an enquiring approach to their learning.

Resources on the CD-ROM

The resources include images of the Qur'an, the 99 names for Allah and the Shahadah. There are also videos showing Muslims demonstrating the prayer positions and explaining the practice of zakat. These resources serve to develop the children's understanding of worship and what it means to belong to a religion.

Photocopiable pages

The photocopiable pages in the book are also provided in PDF format on the CD-ROM and can be printed from there. They include:
▶ word cards containing essential vocabulary for the unit
▶ an activity sheet on guidelines for living from the Hadith
▶ stories about the Prophet Muhammad.

NOTES ON THE CD-ROM RESOURCES

99 names of Allah

Belief in One God, Allah, lies at the heart of Islam. For Muslims, only belief in Allah and his power can explain the wonders of the world, the beauty of nature, the pattern of day passing into night and the changes of the seasons. Muslims believe that all this did not come into being by accident but was, and is, Allah's design for the world. Allah is therefore a Creator. The Qur'an has 99 names for Allah, each telling about the nature of Allah; for example, Allah is the All Merciful, The Protecting Friend, The Guide, The Forgiver, The Source of Peace and The Perfectly Wise.

Discussing the photograph

▶ Talk to the children about how they would describe themselves, a friend or member of their family. How many words would they need to use to do this adequately? Would five or ten be enough?

▶ Discuss the words that a religious person would need to describe God.
▶ Talk with the children about the 99 names for Allah, noting the Arabic script in the photograph.

Activities
▶ Using photocopiable page 47, 'Islam word cards (1)', give each group of children one of the names for Allah. Ask them to discuss meanings for this name, and challenge them to consider why someone who is, for example, a Protecting Friend, would be important for Muslims. Share each group's ideas with the class.
▶ Ask each child to choose one of the names for Allah to copy and decorate with Islamic designs for display alongside the photograph. Invite the children to design a symbol for each of the names. Explain that Allah must not be represented; an example would be a map and compass as a symbol for 'The Guide'.
▶ Invite a Muslim to recite some of the 99 names for Allah in Arabic.
▶ Using a pen with a broad italic nib and Indian ink, try to write Arabic script. Arabic letters are written from the top of the letter, bringing the pen down towards the heart.

The Qur'an

The resource shows an open Qur'an on a Qur'an stand. For Muslims the Qur'an is the Word of Allah, revealed to the Prophet Muhammad through the Angel Jibril. The word 'Qur'an' means 'recitation', for the Prophet was asked to 'recite' the message given to him. The Qur'an is written in Arabic and is divided into 114 sections or surahs; some being short poetic passages, others being longer with guidelines for the worship of Allah and for living. The words in every copy of the Qur'an are exactly the same and have been unchanged since the time of the Prophet. The central teaching of the Qur'an is belief in Allah, but belief has to be followed by actions by each individual in order that a Muslim community might be established. The main teachings concerned with the actions that each individual should follow are usually referred to as the Five Pillars.

Discussing the photograph
▶ Talk with the children about the people or places that they would go to for guidance.
▶ Discuss how many religious people turn to the guidance given in the holy books of their faiths on how they should live their lives. Talk about the authority given to a holy book by believers.
▶ Discuss the types of guidance people might seek from a holy book, for example, how to treat others – even those you do not count as friends.

Activities
▶ Working in groups, ask the children to identify five guidelines that might help people to live together as a community.
▶ Discuss the reasons why or why not people might take the children's guidelines seriously and follow them. Compare this with religious people who follow guidelines which they believe are given by God.
▶ Learn about how the Qur'an was revealed by Allah to the Prophet Muhammad while he was alone in a cave, praying and thinking about Allah.
▶ Learn how a Muslim treats the Qur'an in order to show respect for the book and its message (for example, how it is wrapped up and kept on a high shelf when not being read; and how to read the Qur'an is a form of worship). Further information can be gained from interviewing a Muslim or from a video/DVD such as *Pathways of Belief: Islam* (BBC Education).

The Shahadah, Audio: The Shahadah

The Shahadah – the profession or declaration of faith – is the first of the Five Pillars or duties for every Muslim. The audio clip explains the meaning of the Shahadah, summing up Muslim belief in the one God, Allah, and in Muhammad as the Prophet or Messenger of Allah. The Shahadah can be translated as: 'There is no God except Allah, Muhammad is the Messenger of Allah'.

Discussing the audio clip and photograph

▶ Talk with the children about the ease or difficulty of creating a 'Creed' or 'Declaration' of your most important beliefs in one sentence.

▶ Discuss the sight and sound of the Shahadah in written and aural form.

▶ Discuss the different creeds or statements of faith remembered from different religions, such as the Christian Creed and the Shema from Judaism.

Activities

▶ In groups, ask the children to brainstorm some of their 'secular' beliefs, such as caring for animals or helping the old and the poor. Ask the children to try to summarise these in one or two statements. Share these with the class and display them.

▶ Discuss the meaning of the Shahadah and the similarities and differences between the Shahadah and statements of faith from other religions.

Video: Salah – prayer in Islam

Salah, prayer five times a day, is the second of the Five Pillars of Islam (five duties which every Muslim should perform). In the video a child describes how he prepares for and performs prayer. First he performs wudu, the ritual washing. Then he places his prayer mat towards Makkah, with his hands behind his ears, recites his intention to pray and performs the prayer positions. The prayer positions are bending forward with hands on knees, kneeling and touching the forehead on the prayer mat and finally sitting back on the heels and turning the head from left to right. The demonstration of prayer includes the words *Bismillah-ir-Rahman-ir-Rahim*, 'In the name of Allah – All Gracious, All Merciful', a statement of belief said by Muslims before reading the Qur'an or beginning any action.

Discussing the video

▶ Discuss the different positions that people in different faiths adopt for prayer.

▶ Talk with the children about the reasons why people pray, for example; to ask for help or to worship God.

▶ Discuss how the Muslim child prepares for prayer; how he prays and the words spoken.

Activities

▶ Find pictures in books showing people praying. Discuss the 'clues' in the pictures which show they are praying – the position of the hands and bodies.

▶ Discuss what the child in the video means when he says he is 'submitting' himself to Allah. Consider the position he is in when he says this. Make links between the idea of submission and the actions which reflect this.

▶ Invite a Muslim to talk to the children about why prayer is important in Islam.

Video: What is Zakat?

The video shows a child and his mother discussing zakat, the third of the Five Pillars. Zakat is the collection of money for the poor and needy in the community. Muslims should give 2.5% of their disposable income every year as zakat. By doing this they believe the heart of the contributor is purified from selfishness and greed. The effect of zakat is therefore both personal and communal, for it purifies the giver and contributes to the community.

Discussing the video

▶ Talk to the children about the different charities and appeals they are aware of.

▶ Have the children ever given money to charity? How does it make them feel?

▶ Ask: *How might Akbar feel when he collects pennies in his Zakat box?*

Activities

▶ Ask the children to evaluate the uses of their pocket money into necessities and luxuries. Discuss what it would mean to them and to others to give some of this to charity.

▶ Watch clips of film made for 'Red Nose Day' or other national appeals. Talk about the big effect that people can have (in terms of helping others) if they all give a little money.

▶ With the children's help, identify a charity for the class or school to support for a term. Together organise the methods for collecting funds, sending a letter and cheque or inviting a representative to the school to collect the funds.

▶ If the collection of money is not appropriate, organise for the children to do something practical, such as some gardening for elderly people in the area, or singing at an old people's home, or carrying out simple chores at home or in school.

Ramadan

Fasting during the month of Ramadan is the fourth of the Five Pillars. During this month, Muslims will go without food and drink during the hours of daylight, so they will rise and eat before daybreak and then not eat or drink again until after sunset. The hours of daylight and therefore of fasting will differ for different countries of the world according to whether Ramadan occurs in summer or winter and, as the month is determined by the lunar calendar, the time of Ramadan differs slightly each year.

Ramadan is commanded in the Qur'an. It is a time to think about the spiritual, rather than the physical side of a person; a time for reflecting on Allah and his gifts; a time to increase the study of the Qur'an, and a time to think about those who do not have enough to eat. The picture shows a family sharing food together, possibly before the fast begins at daybreak. The old, sick and very young do not need to fast.

Discussing the photograph
▶ Discuss the times during the day when the children eat and what they eat.
▶ Talk about how the picture shows the family sharing a meal together before the fast begins for the day.

Activities
▶ For one month, make a diary of the times when the sun rises and sets.
▶ Write a diary for a day during Ramadan, noting the sunrise and sunset times, and when meals are allowed. Also remember the five times of prayer for Muslims.
▶ Invite a Muslim to speak to the children about the month of fasting and the meals which are prepared and eaten during the month.
▶ During the month of Ramadan, choose one book which can be read and studied for the month.
▶ Study one of the sayings of Prophet Muhammad (the Hadith) each week and try to put its message into practice (see photocopiable page 49).

Map of Hajj

The hajj or pilgrimage to Makkah is the fifth Pillar. The map shows the position of Makkah in relation to the United Kingdom and an outline of the Great Mosque with the Ka'bah at the centre.

Discussing the map
▶ Identify the places on the map and explain why Muslims make the hajj or pilgrimage to Makkah.
▶ Talk about special journeys and ask the children to point out other places that they may have visited for particular reasons.

Activities
▶ Investigate how easy or difficult it is for Muslims to make hajj to Makkah. Plan a journey to Makkah from the United Kingdom and from one other country. Investigate the mode of travel, the time it takes and the cost. Some travel agents would be able to assist in this exercise. Mark the nearest airport to the local area and the proposed journey on the map.
▶ Display this map when discussing resources on the Ka'bah at Makkah so that the children will understand the geographic location of Makkah.
▶ Ask the children to estimate the distance between Makkah and London, and then find out the actual distance.

NOTES ON THE PHOTOCOPIABLE PAGES

Islam word cards

These cards show key words that children will encounter when working on the unit:
► words relating to the names for Allah
► words to describe the key concepts and Five Pillars in Islam.
Read through the word cards with the children to familiarise them with the key words of the unit. Clarify any words that the children don't understand.

Activities

► Cut out the cards and laminate them. Use them as often as possible when talking about ways in which people can belong to a particular religion, group or organisation.
► Encourage the children to match the word cards to the pictures in the Resource Gallery.
► Use the word cards for displays about the Five Pillars or Duties of a Muslim.

The Hadith

The Hadith are sayings and actions of the Prophet Muhammad, remembered and recorded by his followers. They give Muslims examples of how to behave. Use this activity sheet independently, or as an additional focus when discussing how Muslims should behave. Link it to lessons about giving zakat, or to the stories about the crying camel and the old woman.

Activities

► Cut out the sayings from the photocopiable sheet and give one to each group to discuss the meaning and the implications for daily life.
► Let each group produce a role-play to explain the meaning of their Hadith.
► Compare the Hadith with photocopiable page 29 on the sayings of Jesus. Identify those which are similar in ideas (though the words are different).

Muhammad and the thirsty camel

This story highlights Muslim belief in Allah as the Creator and the responsibility of humans to act as 'caretakers' of all Allah's creations. In the story, the Prophet, in his concern for the camel, shows an example to the men of how they should be concerned about Allah's creatures before being concerned for their own pleasure.

Activities

► Read the story and discuss the reasons why the Prophet Muhammad was so angry with the man who had ignored his camel's welfare.
► Talk with the children about the belief that Allah or God is the Creator, discussing the implications of this for believers – namely their responsibility to care for the world.
► Investigate different organisations that are concerned with the welfare of animals, including those concerned with protecting endangered species.

Muhammad and the old woman

This story illustrates the care and concern the Prophet Muhammad had for all people, regardless of their attitude to him. It also illustrates the belief that we should care for others as they are part of Allah's creation.

Activities

► Talk with the children about their responses when someone is unkind or rude to them.
► Read or tell the story of Muhammad and the old woman and discuss her response to him.
► Talk with the children about how Muhammad's actions changed the woman's attitude. Discuss with them the way in which our responses, even when treated unkindly, can change the pattern of others' actions.

Islam word cards (1)

Allah
Creator
All Merciful
The Protecting Friend
The Guide
The Perfectly Wise
The Source Of Peace
The Forgiver

Islam word cards (2)

Muslim

submission

Shahadah

Ramadan

Hajj

zakat

Qur'an

salah

The Hadith

The Hadith are sayings and actions of the Prophet Muhammad, remembered by his followers. Here are some examples.

THE PROPHET said: 'Righteousness is good character, and sin is what makes you uncomfortable inside, and you would not like other people to find out about.'

THE PROPHET said: 'There is no better gift a parent can give his child than good manners.'

THE PROPHET said: 'When three (or more) people set out on a journey they should choose one of them to be their leader.'

THE PROPHET said: 'The world is green and delightful, and Allah has put you in charge of it, and is watching how you behave.'

THE PROPHET said: 'Do not use any living thing as a target.'

THE PROPHET said: 'Make things easy (for people) and do not make them difficult, and cheer people up and do not put them off (by your behaviour).'

A man once asked the Prophet: 'What is the best thing in Islam?' He replied, 'To feed people, and greet both those you know and those you do not know (with *as-salâmu 'alaykum*).'

THE PROPHET said: 'There are two blessings that many people fail to make the most of: good health and free time.'

These have been selected from *In the Prophet's Garden: A selection of ahadith for the young* compiled by Fatima M. D'Oyen and Abdelkader Chachi (The Islamic Foundation, 2002)

Muhammad and the thirsty camel

One day, the Prophet was walking through the city when he came to a pleasant, shaded garden. Some men were sitting under the leafy trees, others were drinking tea and talking. In one corner of the garden was a camel and it was obvious that the animal was in distress. The thin and exhausted animal was tied to a post in the hot sun and was howling.

Muhammad stroked the camel and talked softly to it. Then he approached the men who were drinking tea and talking. They all were relaxed, enjoying their tea in the shade.

'Whose camel is this?' Muhammad asked.

'It's mine,' replied one of the men.

'You should be ashamed of yourself,' said Muhammad. 'Allah has given you this animal. It has worked for you but you have not taken care of it. This animal is one of Allah's creatures and you have a duty to care for this animal before you relax, take tea and talk with your friends.'

The man was ashamed. From that day onwards, he remembered to look after his animals properly and to give them enough food and drink.

Illustration © Sarah Warburton

SCHOLASTIC
PHOTOCOPIABLE

Muhammad and the old woman

Each day, when Muhammad went to the mosque to pray, he would pass an old woman sweeping the front of her house. The old woman did not like Muhammad and each day she would sweep dust over him as he passed. Muhammad would always say 'Good morning', but the woman never replied.

One day, as Muhammad walked past the old woman's house, he noticed that she was not there sweeping. Muhammad asked the woman's neighbours where she was. They told him that she was ill and unable to do her cleaning. Straightaway, Muhammad went to the old woman's house. He swept and cleaned the house and then cooked the woman a meal. The woman was astonished that someone had come to help her and was even more surprised when she discovered that it was Muhammad. She was ashamed of how she had treated him.

From that day onwards, the old woman changed. She followed the example of Muhammad and was kind and helpful to everyone she met.

Illustration © Sarah Warburton

SCHOLASTIC
PHOTOCOPIABLE

READY RESOURCES ▶▶ RELIGIOUS EDUCATION

HINDUISM

Content and skills

This chapter focuses on the Hindu concept of God and addresses the questions, 'What do Hindus believe about God?'; 'How are these beliefs expressed through visual images?' and 'How do Hindus worship God in the mandir?'. In this chapter aspects of God or the divine, represented in images of Ganesh, Krishna and Shiva are explored. The resources and notes in this chapter link closely with those of Hindu places of worship in Chapter one.

Beliefs about God and community worship in Hinduism (and in other faiths) are important focal points for learning at Key Stage 2 in most LEA Agreed Syllabuses for religious education. These topics are also reflected in the themes of 'beliefs and questions', 'symbols and religious expression' and 'religion, family and community' in the non-statutory framework for religious education.

This chapter encourages children to engage with the concept of God and to explore how this is interpreted and expressed through visual images. The chapter will enable children to develop their religious vocabulary through their discussions about aspects of the divine, develop their understanding of the concept of worship and enable them to recognise and interpret different forms of religious expression.

The Resource Gallery for 'What do Hindus believe about God?' on the CD-ROM, together with the teachers' notes and photocopiable pages in this chapter, support teaching and learning about the Hindu concept of God and Hindu worship. The teachers' notes contain background information about the resources and include ways of using them as a whole class, for group work or as individuals. Some of the activities link with other areas of the curriculum, such as literacy and art and design. Wherever possible, the activities encourage the children to ask questions and develop an enquiring approach to their learning.

Resources on the CD-ROM

The resources include images of Ganesh, Krishna as a baby and as an adult, and Shiva as Lord of the Dance. There are also videos where Hindus explain how and why they worship in the mandir. These resources serve to develop the children's understanding of Hinduism and what it means to belong to a religion.

Photocopiable pages

The photocopiable pages in the book are also provided in PDF format on the CD-ROM and can be printed from there. They include:
▶ word cards containing essential vocabulary for the unit
▶ stories about Ganesh and Krishna
▶ an activity sheet on how to set up a Hindu shrine.

NOTES ON THE CD-ROM RESOURCES

Video: Worship in the mandir

The video shows a Hindu mother and child explaining how they worship in the mandir and why it is important to them. The child explains that first a bell is rung to let the gods know that the worshippers are present. Prayers are then made to Ganesh – the 'Remover of Obstacles' (worshippers ask Ganesh to help them in their worship). The priest performs 'arti', which involves moving the flame in the arti lamp before the deities. In this mandir the lamp is moved before Lord Krishna, asking for his blessings.

Hindus bring offerings, often fruit, to be placed before the deities for blessing. These are then shared with the worshippers as 'prashad', or blessed food. For the Hindu mother and child, worshipping in the mandir is a special social and spiritual time.

Discussing the video clip
▶ Discuss the reasons why the child and the mother like going to the mandir.
▶ Talk about the different activities that the child and the mother do when they go to the mandir.
▶ Discuss those actions that are similar to those in other places of worship and those that are different.

Activities
▶ Discuss the various focal points for worship in different religions. For example, Jews will face towards the Ark with the Sefer Torah; Christians will face towards the altar (or in other churches a cross); Muslims will face towards Makkah. Talk with the children about why these are all different and the associations for the worshippers.
▶ Ganesh is known as the remover of obstacles. Can the children think of any other people that remove obstacles for them? Encourage them to relate some of their own experiences.

Ganesh

Hindus believe in one God, but believe that different aspects are represented through different images: Ganesh is god as the Remover of Obstacles; Lakshmi is the goddess of wealth and good fortune; Shiva is both a destroyer and source of creation.

Ganesh is shown with four arms, a symbol of his power as a god. A right hand is raised in blessing, the bottom left hand holds a sweet (for Ganesh loved sweet things). At Ganesh's feet is a rat upon which he rides; this is a symbol of the interdependence of big and small creatures. The snake around Ganesh's waist and the broken tusk are a reminder of the story when Ganesh was riding on his rat. In the story, a snake slid across Ganesh and the rat's path; the rat came to a sharp halt and Ganesh fell, his stomach bursting open and all the sweet things falling out. Ganesh quickly pushed the sweet things back in, using the snake to hold his stomach together. The moon watching the scene laughed, so Ganesh snapped off his tusk and threw it at the moon.

Ganesh is worshipped prior to any event such as an examination or moving house.

Discussing the photograph
▶ Talk with the children about the image of Ganesh in the photograph.
▶ Discuss how both elephants and rats can remove obstacles in their path.
▶ Discuss why the elephant-headed Ganesh might be a useful image or aspect of God.

Activities
▶ Make images of Ganesh for display; use different media such as collage, clay, paint or mosaic.
▶ Think about the times when Hindus might pray to Ganesh to remove obstacles.
▶ Tell the story of how Ganesh received his elephant head (photocopiable page 59).
▶ Discuss how and when people of other faiths pray to God to help them.

Krishna as a baby

Lord Krishna is depicted both as a child and as an adult. He is the 'playful' aspect of God, as he often gets up to mischief, such as stealing his mother's butter (as shown in the story 'Krishna steals the butter!', photocopiable page 58), and stealing the saris of the gopis (cowherd girls) as they bathe in the river. But Krishna is loved by worshippers and attracts them to worship him. Krishna is often blue, the colour of the sky, reflecting his status as god.

Discussing the photograph
▶ Talk with the children about what they can see and what is happening in this picture.
▶ How do the children feel as they look at God represented as this young child?
▶ Discuss whether the picture and story about stealing the butter is a 'bad' image to have of God.

Activities
▶ Read or tell the story about Krishna stealing the butter (photocopiable page 58).
▶ Discuss the explanation that Hindus give as to why Yashoda could not tie up Krishna.
▶ Use the picture of Krishna as the basis for the children's own observational drawings.

Lord Krishna & Radha, Video: Worshipping Lord Krishna

The picture, set in a mandir, shows a shrine to Lord Krishna and his consort Radha. Krishna is a popular deity and is usually shown playing his flute, the sound of which captivates the women in the villages; they leave their husbands, their children and homes and go to dance in a circle with Krishna. Each person thinks that she alone is dancing with Krishna, but actually Krishna is dancing with them all. This is how worshippers should feel about god – that she or he is special, but the truth is that all are special to God. Radha and Krishna's mutual love is an example of the perfect devotion towards and with God.

The child in the video explains how a 'puja' or worship tray is placed before Krishna; on it are placed a small bowl of water, some fruit, flowers, a lighted diva, incense sticks and a bell. The bell alerts the god to the worshipper; the fruit and flowers come from the earth; the incense sticks perfume the air; and there is water – all the elements being part of the worship.

Discussing the video and photograph
▶ Talk with the children about the images of the deities and the other items seen on the shrines in the video and photograph.
▶ Discuss the 'clues' in the picture that show that these figures are important.
▶ Talk with the children about all the items on the puja tray as described by the Hindu child.

Activities
▶ Tell the children the story about how the sound of Krishna's music attracts the worshippers to him. Discuss the possible reasons why the 'murti' of Krishna with his flute is often represented in mandirs.
▶ Collect the items described on the video for the puja tray.
▶ Visit a mandir to learn about the murtis or deities present there.
▶ Invite a Hindu to speak to the children about how the deities help him or her to worship.

Shiva

The picture shows Shiva Nataraj in the form of Lord of the Dance. Shiva is shown in a circle of flames representing the cycle of creation, destruction and re-creation. In Shiva's upper right hand is an hour-glass drum – sound being a symbol for the creation of the Universe; in his upper left hand, he holds a flame of destruction; his raised lower right hand signifies 'Fear not'; while his lower left arm across his body is a reminder of his son, Ganesh, the 'Remover of Obstacles', with his elephant trunk. Shiva dances on the demon of ignorance (ignorance about God). Shiva's hair flies out like long snakes, yet his face is calm.

Discussing the picture
▶ Talk about all the different symbols that the children can see in this picture of Shiva.
▶ Discuss words to describe the feelings created by this image.
▶ Talk about why ignorance might be depicted as a demon.

Activities
▶ Invite a Hindu to talk to the children about the symbols on the Shiva Nataraj image and the importance of this for Hindus.
▶ Devise a dance sequence to convey the cycle of creation, destruction and re-creation in the natural world, possibly linked to changes in the seasons.
▶ Ask the children to make a collage of Shiva Nataraj, including the symbols represented in his four arms.

NOTES ON THE PHOTOCOPIABLE PAGES

Hinduism word cards

PAGES 56-57

These cards show key words that children will encounter when working on the unit:
▶ words relating to worship in Hinduism
▶ words to describe the different aspects of God.
Read through the word cards with the children to familiarise them with the key words of the unit. Ask which words the children have heard before and clarify any they don't understand.

Activities
▶ Cut out the cards and laminate them. Use them as often as possible when talking about ways in which people can belong to a particular religion, group or organisation.
▶ Encourage the children to match the word cards to the pictures in the Resource Gallery.
▶ Use the word cards for displays about Hindu worship.

Krishna steals the butter!

PAGE 58

Lord Krishna is worshipped by Hindus throughout the world. Krishna is sometimes seen as the 'playful' aspect of God as he is often shown being mischievous – stealing his mother's butter and then, when older, stealing the saris of the gopis (the girls who looked after the cows) when they were bathing in the river. However, Krishna is loved by everyone and attracts people to him; this is one example of how god attracts worshippers to him. In this story, Krishna's love of Yashoda and her love for him exemplify the love between god and the worshipper.

Activities
▶ Read or tell the story of Krishna stealing the butter.
▶ Discuss the explanation of why Yashoda could not tie up Krishna (and the idea that god cannot be 'tied up' or constrained).
▶ Look at the images of Krishna in the Resource Gallery and discuss why he is an attractive image of God.

Ganesh and his elephant head

PAGE 59

There are several stories about how Ganesh received his elephant head. The fact that after receiving his elephant head, Ganesh was restored to life, reflects the idea that Ganesh is known as the Remover of Obstacles. It is to Ganesh that Hindus pray before an important event, such as before performing puja or worship; before an exam; or before moving house. Ganesh is also known as the Lord of Wisdom.

Activities
▶ Read or tell the story about how Ganesh received his elephant head.
▶ Find other stories about Ganesh that reveal his other qualities.
▶ Make links between this and the times when people of other religions pray to God to ask for help in removing obstacles.

A Hindu shrine

PAGE 60

This activity sheet illustrates the items needed for a Hindu shrine. If possible, look at other examples of Hindu shrines; either in videos or in photographs. A shrine can be set up to worship a particular god. For example, a shrine could include an image of Ganesh or of Krishna.

Activities
▶ Use this activity sheet with 'Video: Worship in the mandir' (see above) to list the items needed for a Hindu shrine.
▶ Discuss the items that are placed on a shrine and why they might be significant.
▶ Set up a Hindu shrine in the classroom, using pictures from the Resource Gallery.

Krishna
Ganesh
Shiva
The flute-player
The partner of Radha
The lord of the dance
The remover of obstacles
The lord of wisdom

Hinduism word cards (2)

devotion

offering

shrine

murti

arti

puja

Krishna steals the butter!

Krishna loved sweet things. Most of all he loved the sweet, creamy butter that his mother Yashoda made. Every day, he dipped his fingers into the butter pots and ate more and more butter. Yashoda never had any butter left for cooking.

One day, Yashoda hid the butter pot on the roof, but Krishna spotted it. He climbed on his brother's shoulders, smashed the butter pot with a stone and ate the butter as it poured out of the broken pot. When the brothers had eaten their fill, they shared the remains with the monkeys!

Yashoda tried everything to stop her son from stealing butter. In the end, she fetched some rope to tie up Krishna as a punishment – but the rope was not long enough. She fetched some more rope but still it was too short. Yashoda started to cry and Krishna felt sorry for his mother. 'Don't cry,' he said. 'I know you love me and I love you, so I will take my punishment. Tie me up!' Yashoda tied the rope around Krishna and, to her amazement, it was long enough and there was rope to spare!

Hindus say that Yashoda could not tie up Krishna because he was no ordinary child, but God in human form. No rope is long enough to tie up God! It was only Yashoda's love for Krishna and Krishna's love for her that solved the problem in the end.

Illustration © Sarah Warburton

Ganesh and his elephant head

Parvati was lonely and wanted a child, so she took some soap and some flakes of skin from her body and moulded a beautiful baby boy. Then she breathed air into the baby, and the baby came alive. Parvati was delighted. Her son was called Ganesh.

Parvati's husband, the great god Shiva, had been away for many years travelling the universe. When he came home and tried to enter Parvati's room, Ganesh blocked his way. Ganesh did not recognise his father and Lord Shiva did not recognise his son. In anger, Lord Shiva cut off Ganesh's head with his sword!

Parvati was horrified and upset. Lord Shiva promised to bring back the head of the first creature he could find whose head was facing north, the direction Ganesh was facing when he lost his head. The first creature that Lord Shiva's servants found was an elephant! Lord Shiva placed the elephant's head on his son and Ganesh came alive again.

That is how Ganesh received his elephant head.

Illustration © Sarah Warburton

A Hindu shrine

Hindu shrine set courtesy of Articles of Faith www.articlesoffaith.co.uk. Photograph © Scholastic Ltd.

A Hindu shrine helps to focus a person on worship, using the natural elements and senses. Earth is represented by fruit and flowers; air is represented by the sweet scent of incense; fire is present with the lighted diva lamps. Water is placed in front of the murti. On the shrine, there are things to see, smell and touch. The sound of the bell alerts the god to the worshipper.

Murti (image or statue) of Hindu gods

Bell

Diva lamp

Water pot and spoon

Incense

Red table cloth – a special colour in Hinduism

Flowers and fruit offerings

SIKHISM

Content and skills

This chapter addresses the question, 'How do Sikhs express their beliefs through symbols?'. This chapter focuses on symbols of dress and ritual, especially those associated with the Baisakhi festival and the reading of the Guru Granth Sahib.

Symbolism in religion, particularly in relation to Sikhism, is a focus for learning at Key Stage 2 in most LEA Agreed Syllabuses for religious education. This focus is also reflected in the theme of 'symbols and religious expression' in the non-statutory framework for RE. By completing the work in this chapter, the children will develop their religious vocabulary through discussing and interpreting symbolism. They will also be encouraged to make links between symbols and rituals in Sikhism and those in other religions. Questions of identity, belonging and commitment will be raised.

The Resource Gallery and photocopiable pages for this chapter support teaching and learning about Sikhism. The teachers' notes contain background information about the resources and include ways of using them as a whole class, for group work or as individuals. Some of the activities link with other areas of the curriculum, such as literacy and art and design. Wherever possible, the activities encourage the children to ask questions and develop an enquiring approach to their learning.

Resources on the CD-ROM

The resources include images of artefacts and key figures such as Guru Nanak and Guru Gobind Singh. There are also videos of Sikhs explaining how a Sikh wears the symbols of dress and why these are important forms of expression.

These resources serve to develop the children's understanding of what it means to belong to a religion.

Photocopiable pages

The photocopiable pages in the book are also provided in PDF format on the CD-ROM and can be printed from there. They include:
▶ word cards containing essential vocabulary for the unit
▶ an activity sheet that explores the concept of living up to the symbols of dress.

NOTES ON THE CD-ROM RESOURCES

Guru Nanak and Guru Gobind Singh

Guru Nanak, pictured with the white beard, was the first of the ten human Gurus for Sikhs. Guru Gobind Singh, pictured with a bow and arrows, was the tenth and final human Guru, for, following him, the role of Guru passed to the holy book, the Guru Granth Sahib. The word 'Guru' means 'teacher' and is also a term given to God who is referred to as 'Sat Guru' (true teacher) or 'Waheguru' – 'wonderful Lord'. It is also a term given to the ten human Gurus and to the holy book.

Sikhs tell stories about Nanak being a special child from birth; for example, a wise man predicted that he would teach others about God, and when he was a boy, a cobra raised his hood to protect Nanak from the sun. When he grew up, Nanak would go down to the river to bathe each day before saying his prayers. One day, he did not come back. After three days Guru Nanak returned and said that God had given him a job to do – to travel and teach others about God; and from then on, that is what Nanak did. From this time Nanak became a 'Guru' or teacher. Guru Nanak also taught that everyone, rich or poor, of whatever religion, was equal before God.

Guru Gobind Singh established the Khalsa or Community of Sikhs, and the wearing of the Five Ks as symbols of belonging to the Khalsa. In 1699, in the town of Anandpur in northern India, at the time of the harvest or Baisakhi festival, Guru Gobind Singh addressed all the Sikhs and told them that they had to be brave. He asked who would be willing to die for God. After much hesitation, one man stepped forward; Guru Gobind Singh took him into the tent and reappeared alone with blood on his sword. Then he asked the question again. The crowd was scared but a second man stepped forward, and this was repeated until five men had gone into the tent. Guru Gobind Singh then pulled back the curtain of the tent to reveal all five men, dressed alike in yellow trousers and tunics and carrying long swords. He initiated, or baptised, them into the Khalsa by pouring amrit, sugared water, on to their heads and eyes. He gave all the woman the name 'Kaur' meaning princess and all the men the name 'Singh' meaning 'lion' as a symbol of belonging to the Khalsa.

Discussing the pictures
▶ Talk with the children about what they can see in the pictures of the two Gurus.
▶ Discuss the similarities and differences between the two Gurus.
▶ Discuss how the artist has tried to show the importance of the Gurus in their pictures, for example, through painting them both with halos. Talk about other religious paintings where halos show the importance or 'holiness' of the person depicted.

Activities
▶ Read or tell a story about Guru Nanak. Stories can be found in *A Birthday to Celebrate* by Lynne Broadbent and John Logan, (Times to Remember Series, Canterbury Press) or in the video/DVD *Pathways of Belief: Sikhism* (BBC Education).
▶ Talk with the children about Guru Nanak's teaching about equality (see the notes above and the notes on the Langar (see page 64).
▶ Read or watch on video/DVD the story about Guru Gobind Singh and the formation of the Khalsa. This can be seen on *Pathways of Belief: Sikhism* (BBC Education).
▶ Make a cartoon strip version of the story or record a telling of the story on audio tape. Passages about the Guru should be narrated and not acted out.
▶ Visit a gurdwara, a Sikh temple, or invite a Sikh to speak to the children about Guru Nanak and Guru Gobind Singh.

Video: Turban tying, Amrit

The video shows the tying of the turban and an explanation of the importance of the turban for Sikhs. The turban is not one of the five symbols that should be worn by all Sikhs, but has been worn by Sikhs since the time of Guru Nanak. The speaker makes it clear that Sikhs wearing the turban are representing the Guru and that their actions should also live up to the teaching of the Guru.

Children should be aware that not every male Sikh will choose to wear a turban, and not wearing one does not necessarily make a person less of a Sikh.

This photograph shows the Panj piare or 'five beloved ones', reminiscent of the five men who responded to Guru Gobind Singh's request and came forward to give their lives for God. It was these men who established the Khalsa or community of Sikhs and today five men such as those shown take their place at the head of Baisakhi parades and prepare the amrit or sugar water used to initiate or baptise Sikhs into the Khalsa.

The Panj piare wear the same dress and the 5Ks – a Kara can be seen on two of the men, while a third holds the Kirpan or sword. The amrit is stirred with a Khanda or double-edged sword and this sword forms part of the symbol of Sikhism, shown on the Sikh flag. Sikhs who want to make a personal commitment to Sikh beliefs and practice and to wear the 5Ks take amrit. At this ceremony, sugar water is poured into the cupped hands of the initiate for them to drink, then it is sprinkled on their eyes and hair. Verses written by the Gurus are read and hymns of praise to God are sung.

Discussing the video and photograph
▶ Talk with the children about the different ways in which people are initiated, or confirmed,

into a religion, such as through Bar/Bat Mitzvah or Confirmation.
▶ Discuss the feelings of those Sikhs who are about to make the commitment of taking amrit and the responsibilities upon them.

Activities
▶ Invite a Sikh to speak to the children about the responsibilities of being a baptised Sikh.
▶ Discuss the qualities of a Sikh identified in the video clip about turban tying.
▶ Laminate and display this picture alongside the picture of Guru Gobind Singh to form part of a Baisakhi display.

The Nishan Sahib, The Nishan Sahib and Baisakhi

The first picture shows the Sikh flag, the Nishan Sahib, with the Khanda, the Sikh symbol. The Khanda emblem consists of the double-edged sword (in the centre) – a symbol of defending one's faith by spiritual and physical means if necessary; the Kara or bangle, and two Kirpan or swords on either side of the double-edged sword.

The second picture shows the Nishan Sahib and the lowering of the flagpole at the festival of Baisakhi. At Baisakhi, the covering of the flagpole is removed and the flagpole washed, or cleansed, in yoghurt and water. All members of the Sikh community try to be involved in this ritual as a symbol of renewed commitment to their religion. Once washed, a new covering is placed on the flagpole and it is raised outside the gurdwara once more.

Discussing the photographs
▶ Talk with the children about flags and the symbols on them, such as the Star of David on the Israeli flag.
▶ Discuss the people and activities seen in the second photograph.
▶ Consider together the idea of taking part in the cleansing of the flagpole as a way of renewing commitment to your religion.

Activities
▶ Make a Khanda, a Sikh flag for display. Use a triangular piece of orange card; the Sikh symbols can be traced or cut out separately on pieces of black card and assembled.
▶ Baisakhi is celebrated on 13 April, or the nearest Sunday. Investigate the nearest gurdwara in the area and the Baisakhi activities celebrated there. Use maps, directories or the internet.
▶ Invite a Sikh to speak to the children about the story and celebration of Baisakhi in his or her gurdwara.
▶ Laminate the picture to use as part of a Baisakhi display.

Guru Granth Sahib, the holy book, Guru Granth Sahib being put to bed

The first picture shows the Sikh holy book, the Guru Granth Sahib, being read in the gurdwara. The Guru Granth Sahib is written in Gurmukhi, the written form of Punjabi, and consists of hymns of praise to God – there are no narrative passages. Anyone who can read Gurmukhi can read from the holy book, and before a festival the Guru Granth Sahib is read from beginning to end by a series of readers, each reading for about two hours. It takes forty-eight hours to read the Guru Granth Sahib and this reading is called an Akhand Path. The man shown in the picture is waving a chauri or hair fan over the scriptures as a mark of respect.

The Guru Granth Sahib is treated as a living Guru or teacher and in the evening it is 'put to bed' in a separate bedroom in the gurdwara. The second picture shows the bed for the scriptures which are under the decorated covers.

When visiting a gurdwara and sitting on the floor, the feet should never be placed facing the Guru Granth Sahib and the head should always be covered when in the presence of the holy book.

Discussing the photographs
▶ Talk with the children about the two pictures.
▶ Discuss with the children the signs that indicate that the Guru Granth Sahib is special – for example, the beautiful coverings and the waving of the chauri.

▶ Discuss the authority that the writings in a holy book have for the believers.

Activities
▶ Visit a gurdwara to see a copy of the Guru Granth Sahib.
▶ Use a Sikh website to investigate some of the hymns in the Guru Granth Sahib.
▶ Listen to a 'kirtan', the devotional singing of verses from the Guru Granth Sahib (see Audio: A kirtan below).
▶ Laminate the pictures and use as part of a display of holy books from a range of religions.

Audio: A kirtan, Harmonium and tablas, Video: Harmonium being played, Video: Tablas being played

Music plays an important part in worship in the gurdwara. Kirtans, hymns of praise to God, written in the holy book, the Guru Granth Sahib, are sung by groups of singers. A variety of instruments are played.

Discussing the audio clip and videos and photograph
▶ Talk with the children about the different musical instruments shown in the picture.
▶ Talk with the children about how the instruments are played and the different sounds that are made.
▶ Discuss the different forms of music used for worship in various religions, such as voices, organs and drums.

Activities
▶ Invite a music teacher to demonstrate how the instruments are played.
▶ Encourage some of the children to practise playing the tablas.
▶ Invite a Sikh group to the school, or visit a gurdwara, to listen to the live playing of the tablas and harmonium and the singing of kirtans.

Langar

The picture shows the langar in the gurdwara. Hospitality is an important part of Sikh teaching and everyone who visits a gurdwara, Sikh and non-Sikh, is welcome to share the food prepared in the 'langar' (referring to the kitchen and the food served in it). The preparation and sharing of food in the langar is part of worship, so everyone has their head covered. The food is vegetarian and people are asked to only take what they will eat so as not to waste any. Sharing food together is also a symbol of equality, as when Sikhism began in India the caste system was in place and food could only be shared with members of the same caste. Guru Nanak's teaching about equality is reflected in the sharing of the langar.

Discussing the photograph
▶ Ask the children to think of times when food or fasting is part of religious practice (such as fasting during Ramadan).
▶ Talk with the children about their feelings when they share food together.

Activities
▶ Visit a gurdwara to look at the kitchen or langar area.
▶ Discuss with members of the local Sikh community how they get the food provided in the langar – much will be donated by the worshippers and they will be involved in the preparation of the food.
▶ Plan and prepare a simple vegetarian meal to share in class.

The 5 Ks: Video and Photograph

The Five Ks are five symbols worn by all baptised Sikhs – that is all Sikhs, male and female, who have taken amrit or initiation into the Khalsa. The names of the five symbols all begin with the Punjabi letter K. They are: 'Kesh' the uncut hair and beard – a symbol of holiness;

'Kangha', a wooden comb, worn in the hair to keep it tidy at all times – a symbol of cleanliness; 'Kachera', shorts worn as underwear and a symbol of modesty, 'Kara', a steel bracelet worn at all times as a reminder of the oneness of God; and 'Kirpan', a sword – a symbol of defence and protection, not of attack.

The 5Ks are outward symbols of a Sikh's inner beliefs and a constant reminder of his or her religious commitment. It is the duty of each Sikh to live up to the uniform of the 5Ks in their words and actions.

Discussing the photograph

▶ Talk with the children about their own experiences of wearing uniforms and badges that identify them as members of a community. Discuss their responsibilities as members of the community and the advantages of belonging to a community.

▶ Discuss the picture of the 5Ks and the meanings of the symbols given in the video.

Activities

▶ Make a display of the 5Ks using the photograph and, if possible, some of the actual items. Add captions to the display with explanations of the meaning of the symbols.

▶ Collect a list of words that describe the qualities of a person wearing the 5Ks. For example, 'dedication', 'courage' and 'an honourable character'.

▶ Discuss situations in daily life when a Sikh might have to show some of these qualities and whether it would be easy or difficult.

▶ Read or tell the story of 'The donkey and the tiger skin', see photocopiable page 68 and make links between this story and the wearing of the turban and the 5Ks.

▶ Discuss the wearing of the 5Ks and the wearing of religious symbols in other religions, for example, the Star of David.

NOTES ON THE PHOTOCOPIABLE PAGES

Sikhism word cards

PAGES 66-67

These cards show key words that children will encounter when working on the unit:
▶ words relating to the Sikh symbols
▶ words relating to the Sikh Gurus and to Sikh celebrations.
Read through the word cards with the children to familiarise them with the key words of the unit. Ask which words the children have heard before and clarify any they don't understand.

Activities

▶ Cut out the cards and laminate them. Use them as often as possible when talking about ways in which people can belong to a particular religion, group or organisation.

▶ Encourage the children to match the word cards to the pictures in the Resource Gallery.

▶ Use the word cards for displays about 'Baisakhi' or 'The Sikh Gurus'.

The donkey and the tiger skin

PAGES 68

Sikhs wear the Five Ks as outer symbols of their inner religious beliefs. This story on photocopiable page 68 illustrates that in your actions you should live up to the clothes or symbols you are wearing.

Activities

▶ Discuss how school and club uniforms or badges identify the children as belonging to a group of people. Discuss what is expected of the children when they are wearing these uniforms or badges.

▶ Read or tell the story of 'The donkey and the tiger skin' on photocopiable page 68.

▶ Discuss what might be expected of religious people, from any religion, who wear symbols of their beliefs.

Sikhism word cards (1)

Sikh
turban
the Five Ks
Kesh (uncut hair)
Kangha (comb)
Kara (bracelet)
Kachera (shorts)
Kirpan (sword)

Sikhism word cards (2)

Guru Nanak

Guru Gobind Singh

amrit

Guru Granth Sahib

Nishan Sahib

Baisakhi

kirtan

langar

The donkey and the tiger skin

The potter's donkey had to work hard. All day he had to carry large sacks full of pots through the busy streets of Anandpur. He worked even through the hottest part of the day, but the potter never gave the poor animal any water to drink. Even when he groaned, 'Ee aw, ee aw!' the people just laughed at the poor creature.

Guru Gobind Singh looked sadly at the donkey and thought how different the animal's life would have been if he had been born a tiger. Just then, Guru Gobind Singh thought of a plan! He untied the donkey and placed over its back a tiger skin which he had been carrying.

The donkey, covered in the tiger skin, strolled into the market streets. When the people saw him, they started shouting, 'Help! A tiger!' The donkey began to enjoy himself, eating all he wanted from the market stalls. He was so happy, he started to bray, 'Ee aw! Ee aw!'

The people were astonished. 'It's not a tiger – it's only the potter's donkey,' they cried, and were no longer afraid.

The moral of this story is: If you are wearing the skin of a tiger, don't behave like a donkey!

BUDDHISM

Content and skills

This chapter addresses the questions, 'Who was the Buddha and what did he teach?' and 'How do Buddhists express their beliefs through symbols, and what do the symbols mean?'.

The ideas, discussions and activities in this chapter consider the life of the Buddha; how his enlightenment is interpreted through symbolism in the Buddharupa or image of the Buddha; and how his teaching is expressed through the Five Precepts and the Noble Eightfold Path. The children are encouraged to consider the teachings of the Buddha, the implications of these teachings for Buddhists today and to reflect on the relevance for their own lives.

The Buddha and his teaching will be an area for learning at Key Stage 2 in many, although not all, LEA Agreed Syllabuses for RE and these areas are reflected in themes in the non-statutory framework for Religious Education, specifically through the themes of 'inspirational people', 'teachings and authority' and 'symbols and religious expression'.

By completing the work in this chapter, the children will develop their religious vocabulary and their ability to describe beliefs and teachings; they will develop their ability to make links between the teachings of different religions and to suggest meanings for different types of religious symbolism and expression.

The Resource Gallery on the CD-ROM for this chapter, together with the teachers' notes and photocopiable pages, support teaching and learning about Buddhism. The teachers' notes contain background information about the resources and include ways of using them as a whole class, for group work or as individuals. Some of the activities link with other areas of the curriculum, such as literacy and art and design. Wherever possible, the activities encourage the children to ask questions and develop an enquiring approach to their learning.

Resources on the CD-ROM

The resources include images of the Buddha, the celebration of Buddhist festivals and Buddhist symbols. There is also a video of a Buddhist explaining how Buddhists interpret and practise the Five Precepts and activity sheets on the life of the Buddha and the Noble Eightfold Path. These resources serve to develop the children's understanding of Buddhism, and what it means to be a Buddhist.

Photocopiable pages

The photocopiable pages in the book are also provided in PDF format on the CD-ROM and can be printed from there. They include:

▶ word cards containing essential vocabulary for the unit
▶ activity sheets that explore the life of the Buddha
▶ an activity sheet on what it means to practise the Noble Eightfold Path
▶ an activity sheet showing mudras and symbols in Buddhism
▶ an activity sheet describing a Buddhist shrine.

NOTES ON THE CD-ROM RESOURCES

Small Buddha statue

The picture shows a small Buddharupa or Buddha image, with the Buddha seated in the lotus position on a lotus flower base. The lotus flower grows from roots submerged in mud, up through the clear waters to emerge as a beautiful bloom on the surface. The lotus is an analogy for human development, from beginnings based in ignorance and concern with material things, through the waters of life's experience, to emerge as an enlightened soul, like the lotus. The Buddha's curled hair is a symbol of a great man, with the 'bump' on his head representing wisdom. The hand gestures, or mudras, are also symbolic and here, the left hand resting in the lap with the right hand touching the earth is a call to the earth to witness the Buddha's enlightenment, and his resolve to help other living things.

Discussing the photograph
▶ Talk with the children about what they can see in the picture.
▶ Discuss the atmosphere, or feeling, evoked by the Buddha seated in this position. Does the Buddha seem calm or worried?
▶ Talk with the children about why a key figure might be shown in this way, and the message this might have for the Buddha's followers.

Activities
▶ Make Buddharupas from modelling clay, focusing on the position of the hands. Use the illustrations of mudras (hand positions) found on photocopiable page 78 as inspiration for the design.
▶ Practise sitting in the lotus position with legs crossed. This is a position where the body is perfectly balanced, representing the balance of mind after following the Noble Eightfold Path.
▶ Visit a Buddhist temple or Meditation Centre to look at and learn more about the Buddharupas.
▶ Invite a Buddhist to speak to the children about how he or she follows the Buddha's example by meditating.

Video: What do Buddhists promise?

The Buddhist in the video explains the meaning of the Five Precepts, or guidelines, given by the Buddha and gives examples of how the Precepts apply in daily life. The Buddha taught that, if people want to be happy, they need to be kind and that following the Precepts is a way of leading a kind and happy life.
The Five Precepts can be paraphrased as:
▶ not to harm other living things
▶ not to take things which have not been freely given
▶ not to be greedy, particularly in relationships with others
▶ to talk kindly and truthfully and not to tell lies
▶ to avoid drugs and alcohol which cloud the way you think and act.

Discussing the video
▶ Talk to the children about guidelines that help people to live a kind and happy life.
▶ Together, identify and discuss the Five Precepts that are explained in the video.
▶ Talk with the children about the Precepts that they think are easy to follow and those which they think they might find difficult.

Activities
▶ Ask the children to work in small groups to brainstorm what they believe should be the five guidelines for a happy life. Compare and discuss the guidelines selected.
▶ Compare the children's responses with the Five Precepts of Buddhism.
▶ Choose one of the Five Precepts as a target for a week. Discuss with the children how they will put the Precept into action during the week, both at home and at school.
▶ Invite a Buddhist to speak to the children about the Five Precepts and how he or she puts them into action in their life.

Wesak – a Buddhist festival

This photograph of a shrine or meditation room in a large Buddhist Centre is decorated to celebrate Wesak, the Buddha's birthday. The festival of Wesak commemorates the Buddha's birth, enlightenment and death.
Different Buddhist communities will mark the festival in different ways. In the temple,

decorations may be put up and paper lanterns lit as a symbol of enlightenment. Buddhists will gather in the temple, provide food for the monks and listen to sermons about the Buddha and his teaching.

To the left of the photograph there are two Buddhist monks visible – members of the Buddhist sangha or community. They are dressed in saffron robes. Behind them is the shrine, not completely visible – but the fresh flowers and candles can be seen. The fresh flowers remind Buddhists that, although beautiful they will change and decay, like everything in the world. The understanding that everything changes is an important teaching of the Buddha. The light of the candles represents the light of the Buddha's teaching and reminds Buddhists that they must put that teaching into action in their own lives.

The hand positions of the congregation suggest that they are paying respect to the Buddha and to the monks for their teaching. Everyone brings food and other necessities, as the monks rely on the generosity of the lay community. Bringing gifts shows loving-kindness on the part of the giver.

Discussing the photograph

▶ Talk with the children about the responsibilities of belonging to a community – how people take different roles and responsibilities.

▶ Look at the photograph and talk about what the children can see happening in this community of Buddhists.

▶ Discuss the different roles of the monks and of the lay community. Ask the children to consider how they support each other – the monks by teaching, and the lay community by providing food for the monks.

Activities

▶ Create a Buddhist shrine in the classroom. See photocopiable page 80, 'A Buddhist shrine'.

▶ Discuss the symbolism of the items on the shrine, for example, the fresh flowers, the incense and the candles.

▶ Visit a Buddhist community to learn the basic skills of meditation: either of sitting very still and focusing on breathing, or of a walking meditation.

▶ Attempt some mirroring exercises. The skills of concentration, so important in Buddhism can be learned from simple mirroring exercises. Work in pairs, standing facing one another, one person starts moving very slowly, perhaps moving just one hand at first and his or her partner tries to follow, mirroring each movement.

▶ Discuss the needs of a community, whether religious or secular. Talk about both the practical and spiritual needs of people in a community. Relate this to the class and discuss what each person can offer their fellow pupils.

Prayer flags in the mountains, A prayer flag

The pictures show Tibetan prayer flags. These are coloured flags in yellow, green, red, white and blue which fly from houses and trees and even from high mountains in Tibet and in other countries such as in parts of Nepal.

The Tibetan name for these flags is 'wind-horse' because each flag has a galloping horse in its centre, with three jewels on its back. The three jewels are not literally jewels but a symbol of three 'tear drops' surrounded by a flame. They refer to the three 'jewels' or important elements in Buddhism, the Buddha, the Dhamma (the teaching of the Buddha) and the sangha (the community of Buddhists). Around the horse are prayers written in Tibetan writing and, as the flags flutter in the wind, the wind carries the prayers, for peace and good things, to all living things.

Discussing the photographs

▶ Talk with the children about flags and the images on the single prayer flag.

▶ Talk with the children about the different ways in which people pray or ask for good things for others – for example, some people will light candles as they say a prayer, or light incense sticks.

▶ Discuss with the children the different wishes or prayers which they might like to make for others.

Activities

▶ Ask the children to work in small groups to brainstorm a list of ideas of wishes that could be made for others.

▶ Discuss whether the children believe that making wishes or saying prayers for others makes a difference to them.

▶ Make a prayer flag using squares of blue, white, red, yellow or green paper. Draw a picture of the wind-horse in the middle of the flag, with the three jewels on its back, and surround it with wishes for all living things, such as: 'Be happy'; 'Be kind' and so on.

▶ Attach the children's flags to a length of string and suspend them across the classroom so that they can flutter in the wind.

NOTES ON THE PHOTOCOPIABLE PAGES

Buddhism word cards PAGES 74–75

These cards show key words that children will encounter when working on the unit:
▶ words relating to the Buddha's life and teachings
▶ words about Buddhist symbols and practice.

Read through the word cards with the children to familiarise them with the key words of the unit. Ask which words the children have heard before and clarify any they don't understand.

Activities

▶ Cut out the cards and laminate them. Use them as often as possible when talking about ways in which people can belong to a particular religion, group or organisation.

▶ Encourage the children to match the word cards to the pictures in the Resource Gallery. Play games of matching words and pictures together.

▶ Use the word cards for displays about 'The Buddha and his teaching'.

▶ Challenge the children to use a word processor and printer to create a set of their own Buddhist word cards relating to the work in this chapter, or Buddhism in general.

Prince Siddhattha — The Buddha, Prince Siddhattha and the Four Sights PAGES 76–77

This story tells about the change in Prince Siddhattha's life from a prince who lived in luxury in the palace to the life of a wandering teacher.

Activities

▶ Talk with the children about their ideal life; where would it be lived and how? Remind them of how Buddhism teaches to guard against materialism. Explain what materialism means and ask the children to consider whether their dreams are materialistic in any way.

▶ Read or tell the story about Prince Siddhattha.

▶ Discuss the reasons why anyone might give up a life of luxury. Do the children think they could give up their toys or other favourite possessions?

▶ Look at the Buddha's teaching of the Noble Eightfold Path (see photocopiable page 79).

▶ Brainstorm the children's ideas of the important things in life. Interview other children and adults to compare responses.

Mudras and symbols in Buddhism PAGE 78

Buddhism is rich in symbols. This activity sheet includes examples of hand gestures (or mudras) used in images of the Buddha to represent different aspects of the Buddha's life and aspects of his teaching. It also includes the symbol of the lotus and the eight-spoked wheel.

Activities

▶ Ask the children to practise the different hand gestures or mudras, using the examples on the activity sheet as a guide. When they have mastered the gestures, ask one child to mime

72

READY RESOURCES ▶▶ RELIGIOUS EDUCATION

the gesture while others guess the meaning.

▶ Make a chart of the different mudras to display around a large image of the Buddha, a Buddharupa (such as that from Chapter 1, page 16).

▶ Create a large collage of the lotus flower symbol for the classroom wall. Display words and phrases around the different parts of the flower to make links with the experience of human development, for example: 'wanting a new bike' (in the muddy waters); 'growing up' (in the clearer waters); 'thinking about others' (near the blooming lotus flower).

▶ On the classroom wall display a large wheel with eight spokes. On each spoke, attach one of the statements from the Noble Eightfold Path (see photocopiable page 79) or translate the statement into 'pupil speak' before displaying it.

The Noble Eightfold Path   PAGE 79

The Noble Eightfold Path is the Buddha's 'prescription' or teaching for a good life. Each of the eight statements has many meanings and applications, both for children and adults.

Activities

▶ In groups, ask the children to discuss the meanings of the eight statements and to write the meanings in the boxes provided. Hold a feedback session where the responses of the groups are shared with the rest of the class.

▶ Ask each group to role-play one of the eight statements to explain how it applies in different situations.

▶ Cut up each of the statements and ask the children to divide them into those which they think would be easy to follow and those which they think would be difficult. Discuss the responses of the groups.

▶ Compare the eight statements with the teachings from other religions. For example, the teachings of Jesus or the sayings from the Hadith. Discuss any that are similar and any that are different.

A Buddhist shrine   PAGE 80

There is a Buddhist shrine in the Meditation Room in Buddhist temples and most Buddhists will have a small shrine in their homes. An example of a home shrine was included in the resources for chapter 1. The shrine will have a Buddharupa or image of the Buddha and other symbols to remind Buddhists of the Buddha's teaching. These items include candles as a reminder of the Buddha's enlightenment, fresh flowers and fruit as a reminder that living and beautiful things all wither and die, incense sticks as a reminder of the sweetness of the Buddha's teaching and water as a symbol of purity.

Activities

▶ Use the photocopiable activity sheet as a checklist for the items that need to be collected for the Buddhist shrine.

▶ Ask the children to select a calm or 'quiet' part of the classroom in which to set up the shrine.

▶ Set up the Buddhist shrine in the classroom and remind the children to check the flowers and fruit for the early signs of decay.

▶ While sitting near the shrine, if possible in the lotus position, read or tell the story of the Buddha's life (see photocopiable page 76) or discuss some of the things he taught, such as the Five Precepts or the Noble Eightfold Path.

Prince Siddhattha

The Buddha

The Four Sights

The Five Precepts

The Noble Eightfold Path

The eight-spoked wheel

enlightenment

The dhamma

Buddhism word cards (2)

respect

meditation

loving kindness

concentration

lotus

prayer flags

suffering

sangha

Prince Siddhattha – the Buddha

When Prince Siddhattha was born, a wise man, Asita, told the King that his son would either be a King or a wandering teacher. King Suddhodana was worried: he wanted his son to stay in the palace for ever. He gave his son everything he could wish for!

As he grew up, Prince Siddhattha grew bored with his life of luxury. One day, his charioteer, Chana, took Siddhattha outside the palace gates. On the road, Prince Siddhattha saw an old man. 'Who is that?' he asked Chana. Chana explained that it was an old man. On a second visit outside the palace, Prince Siddhattha saw a sick man, and on a third visit, he saw a dead man. Prince Siddhattha was shocked when Chana explained that age, sickness and death happen to every living thing. When Chana drove Siddhattha outside the palace gates a fourth time, Siddhattha saw a holy man dressed in saffron robes. He had left his family and all his belongings to live a simple life, trying to understand what life is all about. He looked calm and wise.

Prince Siddhattha decided to follow the example of the holy man. He left his wife, his parents and the palace for a life of meditation. After many years, Prince Siddhattha came to understand important lessons about life. He spent his time travelling and teaching others. He became known as the Buddha, the Enlightened One!

Illustration © Sarah Warburton

■ SCHOLASTIC
PHOTOCOPIABLE

Prince Siddhattha and the Four Sights

Prince Siddhattha in the palace

An old man

A sick man

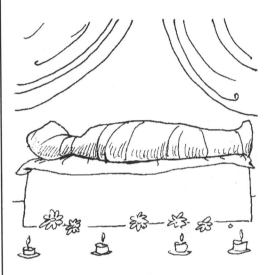

A dead man

A monk

Prince Siddhattha became known as the Buddha after enlightenment.

Illustrations © Sarah Warburton

Mudras and symbols in Buddhism

Statues often show Buddha with different hand positions. These gestures are called mudras and each mudra has a special meaning. Here are some examples.

Meditation
The hands are folded in the lap, palm up with the thumbs joined to form a circle.

Turning the wheel of dhamma
The wheel represents the Buddha's teachings, the dhamma. The eight spokes of the wheel represent the Noble Eightfold Path. In this position, the thumb and index finger are joined to form a circle, a reminder of the wheel of dhamma.

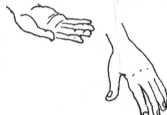

Touching the Earth
The left hand rests in the lap, while the right hand touches the ground, calling the Earth to witness the Buddha's enlightenment and his wish to help others.

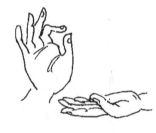

Turning the wheel of dhamma while in meditation
The position of the right hand stands for turning the wheel of dhamma, while that of the left hand symbolises meditation.

The lotus and the eight-spoked wheel have special meanings in Buddhism.

Lotus
From its roots in the mud, the lotus grows upwards through the water and, in the light, blossoms on the surface of the water. For Buddhists, a person's mind is like muddy waters, thinking only of material things, but this can change, as the person moves through the waters of life, and emerges like a beautiful lotus after following the Buddha's teachings.

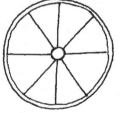

The wheel of life
The wheel is a symbol of a person moving through life. It also represents the Noble Eightfold Path, which guides a person through life to enlightenment – learning the truth about life.

Illustrations © Sarah Warburton

■SCHOLASTIC
PHOTOCOPIABLE

The Noble Eightfold Path

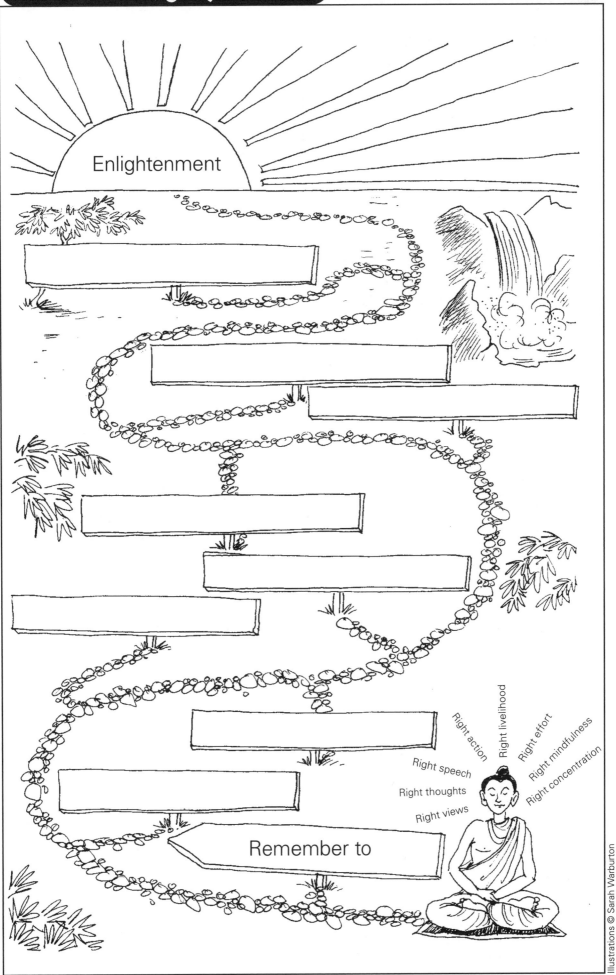

Enlightenment

Right livelihood
Right effort
Right mindfulness
Right concentration
Right action
Right speech
Right thoughts
Right views

Remember to

A Buddhist shrine

The items on a Buddhist shrine give you the opportunity to respect and reflect on the Buddha's teachings.

- A statue of the Buddha – place this at the top of your shrine.

- Candles – they represent an enlightened state. Buddha advised, 'Be unto yourself your own light.' This means that Buddhists have to achieve enlightenment for themselves, using the Buddha's teaching as a guide.

- Water – this represents many things, such as purity and the flow of life.

- Flowers – these reminds us that living things do not last forever.

- Fruit – offerings of food also remind us that living things do not last forever because the food cannot stay fresh and will eventually decay.

- Incense – the sweet smell represents the sweetness of the Buddha's teachings.

■ SCHOLASTIC
PHOTOCOPIABLE